Contents

SNAPREVISE

SNAPREVISE

Energy stores and systems

- A system is an object or a group of objects, such as a kettle filled with water.
- Energy is stored in a system and can take numerous forms. Changes that occur in a system will change how the energy is stored in it.

Types of energy store	
Energy	**Description**
Kinetic	The energy that causes an object to move.
Thermal	The energy that causes objects to become hotter.
Electric	The energy transferred by an electric current.
Chemical	The energy stored in batteries and fuels.
Nuclear	The energy stored in nuclei to hold atoms together.
Gravitational potential	The energy an object gains as it travels upward away from the Earth.
Elastic potential	The energy an object gains as it is stretched or compressed.
Magnetic potential	The energy an object gains due to the magnetic attraction or repulsion it is experiencing.

Conservation and dissipation of energy

- The principle of conservation of energy states that energy cannot be created or destroyed, only transferred.
- Energy can be transferred from one form to multiple others in a system. Dissipated or wasted energy is the energy that has transferred into a form that isn't useful.
- Heat losses can often be reduced using thermal insulation.
  - Thermal conductivity is the rate at which heat is transferred through a material.
  - Insulators have very low thermal conductivities.
- Ways of reducing energy losses are present in many parts of everyday life.
  - Buildings use thick, insulating walls and double glazed windows to keep heat inside.
  - Cars are streamlined to reduce heat lost to air resistance.

Energy calculations

- Energy is measured using the unit Joules, J.
- The kinetic energy of a moving object is $0.5 \times \text{mass} \times (\text{speed})^2$. This can be written as $E_k = \frac{1}{2}mv^2$ where:
  - E_k is the kinetic energy in J
  - m is the object's mass in kg
  - v is the object's speed in m/s.
- The elastic potential energy stored in a spring that has been stretched is given by $0.5 \times \text{spring constant} \times (\text{extension})^2$. This can be written as $E_e = \frac{1}{2}ke^2$ where:
  - E_e is the elastic potential energy in J
  - k is the spring constant of the spring in N/m
  - e is the extension of the spring in m.
- The gravitational potential energy stored in an object raised above ground level is given by $\text{mass} \times \text{gravitational field strength} \times \text{height}$. This can be written as $E_p = mgh$ where:
  - E_p is gravitational potential energy in J
  - m is the mass of the object in kg
  - g is the gravitational field strength in N/kg
  - h is the height raised in m.
- The energy transferred due to a temperature change is given by $\text{mass} \times \text{specific heat capacity} \times \text{temperature change}$. The specific heat capacity of a substance is the energy to raise the temperature of one kilogram of the substance by one degree Celsius. This equation can be written as $\Delta E = mc\Delta\theta$ where:
  - ΔE is the thermal energy transferred in J
  - m is the mass of the object heated or cooled in kg
  - c is its specific heat capacity of the object in J/kg °C
  - $\Delta\theta$ is the temperature change in °C

Power

- Power is the rate at which energy is transferred or at which work is done.
- Power is measured in Watts, W.
- One Watt is the power that would transfer one Joule of energy in one second.
- The power of a process can be calculated as $\text{energy transferred} \div \text{time}$ or $\text{work done} \div \text{time}$. This can be written as $P = \frac{E}{t}$ or $P = \frac{W}{t}$ where:
  - P is the power in W
  - E is the energy transferred in J
  - t is the time taken in s
- If two processes transfer the same amount of energy, then the one that completes the process in less time has a greater power.

Renewable energy and efficiency

Energy resources

- Energy resources are used for transport, heating and electricity generation.
- Most forms of transport, such as cars and planes, are designed to run on fuel. Some cars and trains can run on electricity instead.
- **Renewable resources** (e.g. solar, wind, hydroelectric, tidal, geothermal, biomass) can be replenished naturally and are generally more sustainable.
- **Non-renewable resources** (e.g. coal, oil, natural gas, nuclear fuels) are finite and will eventually run out.

	Resource	Description	Uses
Non-renewables	Fossil fuels (coal, oil, and natural gas)	Stores of energy found underground, which take millions of years to form.	Transport, electricity, heating
	Nuclear power	The process of extracting the nuclear energy in uranium and plutonium.	Electricity
Renewables	Biofuel	The energy gained from burning waste products, such as wood.	Electricity, heating
	Wind	The energy generated from wind turning a wind turbine.	Electricity
	Hydro-electricity	The energy generated from water flowing downhill, often from a high lake behind a dam and turning a turbine.	Electricity
	Geothermal	The energy generated using the heat inside the Earth.	Electricity, heating
	Tidal	The energy generated from water flowing through a turbine as the tides change.	Electricity
	Solar	The energy gained from sunlight through the use of solar panels.	Electricity
	Wave	The energy gained from water waves flowing through a turbine.	Electricity

- Energy mix decisions depend on factors like cost, reliability, environmental impact, and political considerations. For example, approximately 50% of the UK's energy was generated by fossil fuels in 2015, but this value decreased to 27.2% in 2025. Renewables now make up approximately 41% of the UK's energy mix with the majority of this coming from wind power.

Efficiency

- The efficiency of an energy transfer is a unitless number that describes the proportion of energy that is transferred to a useful form. It can be written as a decimal or a percentage.
- Efficiency can be calculated as useful output energy ÷ total input energy.
- Efficiency can also be calculated as useful output power ÷ total input power.
- Efficiency can be increased by reducing energy losses.
  - Reducing the effects of friction through lubrication, reducing heat loss through insulation or reducing the effects of air resistance through streamlining will reduce the energy dissipated to the surroundings.

Energy and the environment

- Fossil fuels will eventually run out in the next 100 years, meaning we will eventually have to switch to renewable energy resources.
- A nuclear power plant can generate much more energy than a fossil fuel power station. The resources for it are expected to last for thousands of years despite being non-renewable.
- The burning of fossil fuels causes carbon dioxide to be released into the environment, contributing to global warming.
  - Nuclear power produces no pollutant gases. However, it does produce radioactive nuclear waste, which needs to be stored safely.
  - Coal will also release sulfur dioxide when burned, which is a cause of acid rain.
  - Bio-fuels are carbon neutral, as the carbon dioxide they release is the same as that taken in before their use as a fuel.

- Power stations can have a negative effect on the areas where they are constructed.
  - Wind turbines can be loud and potentially harmful to birds.
  - Hydro-electric dams will cause a new lake to form behind them. This can destroy natural habitats and force people to move homes.
- Renewable energy resources, such as wind and solar, are entirely weather-dependent. Many countries have systems that switch from these resources to fossil fuels when renewable energy isn't available.

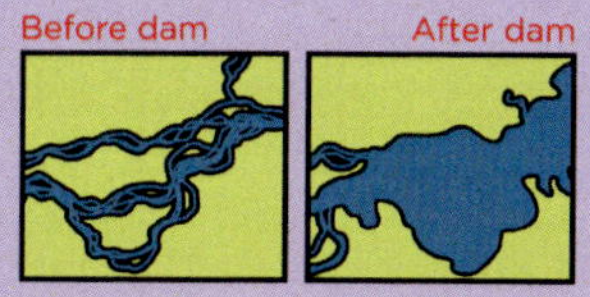

Circuits

Key concepts of circuits

- **Current (*I*)** is the flow of electric charge, measured in **amperes (A)**.
- **Voltage (potential difference, *V*)** is the energy transferred per unit charge, measured in **volts (V)**.
- **Resistance (*R*)** opposes current flow and is measured in **ohms (Ω)**.
- **Charge (*Q*)** is measured in **Coulombs (C)** and calculated as $Q = I \times t$.
- Circuits contain a variety of components:
    - **Switch:** a device used to open and close a circuit, allowing or stopping the flow of current. If the switch is open, the circuit is broken and current cannot flow.
    - **Cell/battery:** provides energy to push charge around the circuit.
    - **Ammeter:** measure the electric current flowing through a circuit, in amperes. It is always connected in series with the component being measured.
    - **Voltmeter:** measures potential difference (voltage) across two points in a circuit. It is always connected in parallel with the component being measured.
    - **Resistor:** limits the current in a circuit.
    - **Variable resistor:** allows current to be adjusted by changing resistance.
    - **Fuse:** a safety device containing a thin wire that melts and breaks the circuit if the current exceeds a certain limit, protecting components from damage or fire.
    - **Lamp:** produces light when current passes through it.
    - **Diode:** allows current to flow in one direction only.
    - **LED:** emits light when current flows through it in the correct direction.
    - **Thermistor:** resistance decreases as temperature increases (used in thermostats).
    - **LDR (Light Dependent Resistor):** resistance decreases as light intensity increases.

Circuit diagrams

Circuit diagrams use symbols and lines to show the components in a circuit and how they are connected.

Symbol	Component
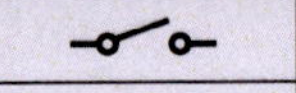	Switch (open)
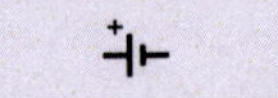	Cell
	Ammeter
	Resistor
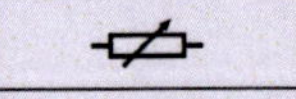	Variable resistor
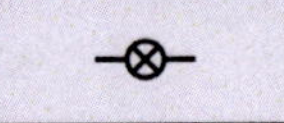	Lamp
	Diode

Symbol	Component
	Switch (closed)
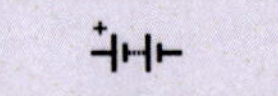	Battery
	Voltmeter
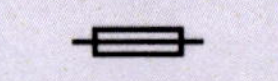	Fuse
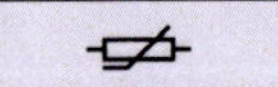	Thermistor
	Light-dependent resistor (LDR)
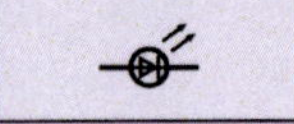	Light-emitting diode (LED)

Series circuits

- Components connected in series are all part of the same branch of a circuit.
- The current through each component will be the same.
- The potential difference will be split between components dependent on their resistances.
    - The total potential difference across the components must be equal to that of the power supply: $V_{supply} = V_1 + V_2$.
    - When connecting cells and batteries in series, the power supply is the sum of their potential differences as long as they are all directed the same way.
- The total resistance, in Ω of two components connected in series is given as $V_{total} = R_1 + R_2$. Connecting resistors in series will increase the total resistance and reduce the current through them.

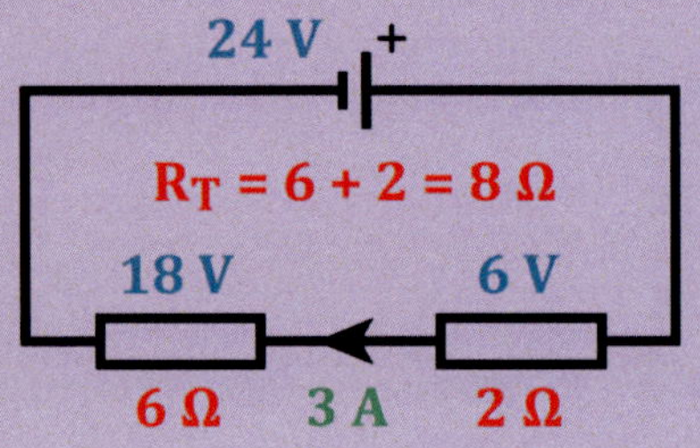

Parallel circuits

- Components connected in parallel are all on separate branches that meet at the same point.
- The potential difference across each component will be the same.
- The current will be split between the branches dependent on their resistances. The current through each component on the same branch will be the same.
- The total resistance of two components connected in parallel will be less than that of the smaller of their resistances.
- Connecting resistors in parallel will reduce the total resistance of the circuit and increase the total current flowing.

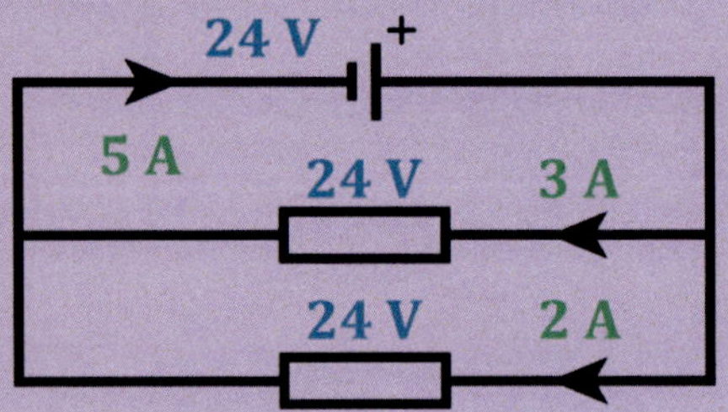

Charge, current, and electric fields

Charge and current

- Electrical charge is an intrinsic property of particles.
  - Protons have a positive charge while electrons have a negative charge.
  - Opposite charges will attract while like charges will repel.
  - Charge is measured in Coulombs, C.
- An electric current is a flow of electrical charge. In circuits, this is the flow of free electrons in wires and components.
  - The current will be the same at any point in a single closed loop.
  - The direction of the current is shown as the opposite to the direction of electron flow.

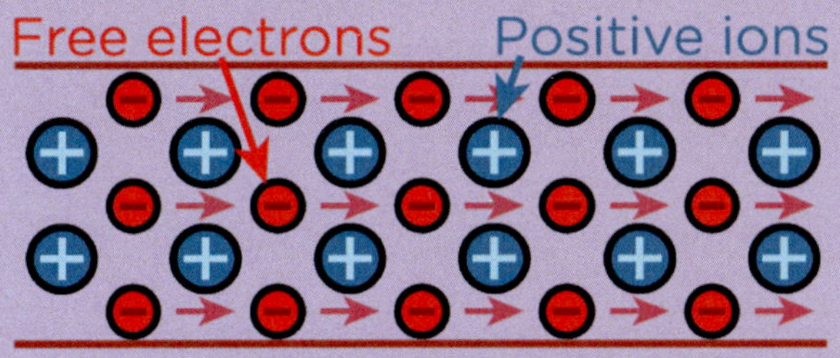

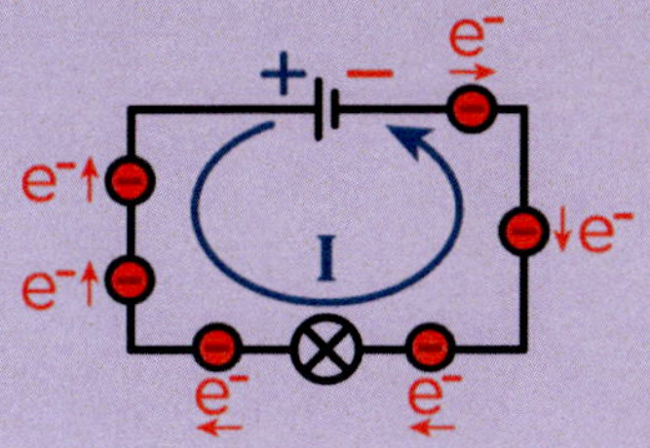

- The size of an electric current is given as the rate of flow of charge. The charge transferred by a current is given as $\text{current} \times \text{time}$.
  - Current is measured in amperes, A.
  - This equation can also be written as $Q = It$ where:
  - Q is the charge in C
  - I is the current in A
  - t is the time in s

Static charge

All specs except: WJEC, CCEA

- When certain insulating materials are rubbed together, electrons will transfer from one material to the other.
  - This produces a static charge in both objects.
  - The object which gains electrons becomes negatively charged while the object which loses electrons becomes positively charged. These charges are equal and opposite.

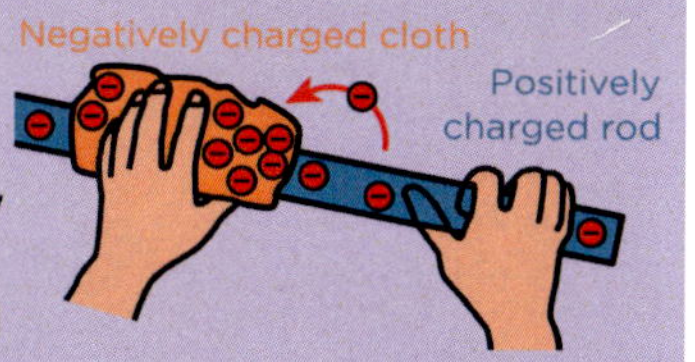

- Two charged objects will attract each other when they have opposite charges and repel each other when they have like charges.
- A spark is produced when a current flows from a charged object to an earthed metal object.

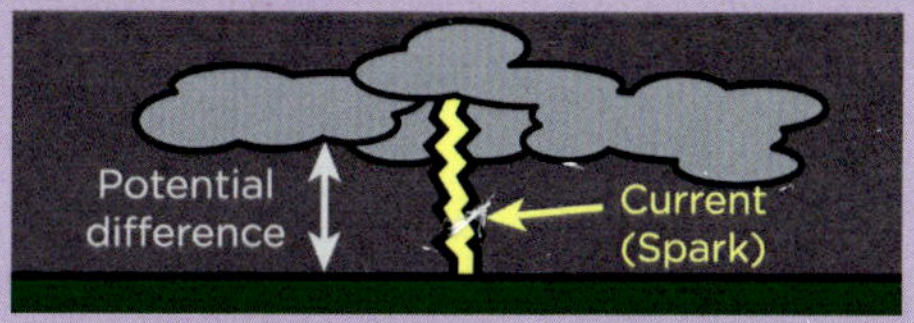

- Thunder clouds are examples of static electricity on a large scale.
  - Clouds gain charge when ice crystals in them rub together.
  - The bottom of the cloud gains a large negative charge.
  - Lightning is a spark between the cloud and the Earth due to a potential difference of millions of volts between them.

Electric fields

All specs except: WJEC, CCEA

- A charged object will create an electric field around itself.
  - This field is strong close to the object and weakens with distance from the object.
  - Increasing the charge of the object will also increase the strength of the field.
- A charged object in the field will experience a non-contact force.
  - This will be an attractive force for opposite charges and repulsive for like charges.
  - The strength of the force is dependent on the strength of the field.
- Electric fields can be shown using field lines.
  - The field lines point in the direction of the force that a positively charged object would experience in the field.
  - The field lines get further apart with distance from the object because the field becomes weaker.

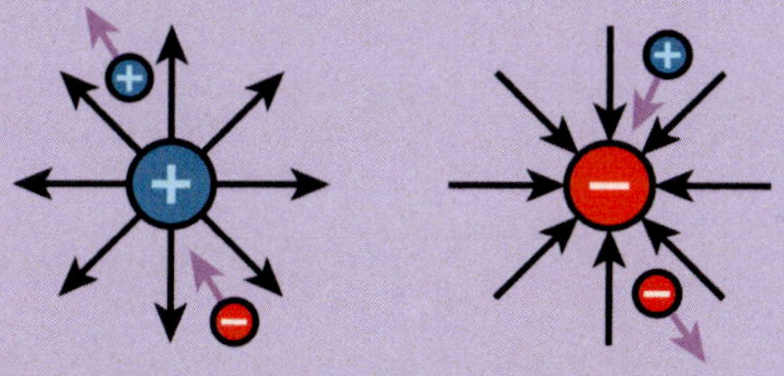

Potential difference and resistors

Potential difference and resistance

- A current will only flow through a circuit when it has a source of potential difference (sometimes called a voltage). This will typically be provided by a cell or battery.
  - The electrons in the circuit are repelled from the negative terminal of the cell and attracted towards the positive terminal.
  - Potential difference is a measure of the electrical work done to move charge carriers through the circuit. It is measured in volts, V.
- Resistance is a measure of how difficult it is to form a current for a particular potential difference.
  - Resistors are used in circuits to decrease the current through the whole circuit or in certain parts of it.
  - Resistance is measured in Ohms, Ω.
- Current, potential difference and resistance in a component are related by the equation $\text{potential difference} = \text{current} \times \text{resistance}$. This can also be written as $V = IR$ where:
  - V is the potential difference across the component in V
  - I is the current in A
  - R is the resistance in Ω

Measuring resistance

- The current through a component can be measured using an ammeter.
  - This must be connected in series with the component.
  - Ammeters have very low resistance so that they don't change the current in the circuit.
- The potential difference across a component can be measured using a voltmeter.
  - This must be connected in parallel with the component.
  - Voltmeters have very high resistances so that very little current flows through them.
- The resistance of a component can be found by measuring the current through it and potential difference across it.
  - A variable resistor can also be used to vary the current through the component.
  - By taking potential difference readings for multiple currents, it can be determined how the resistance changes for non-ohmic conductors.

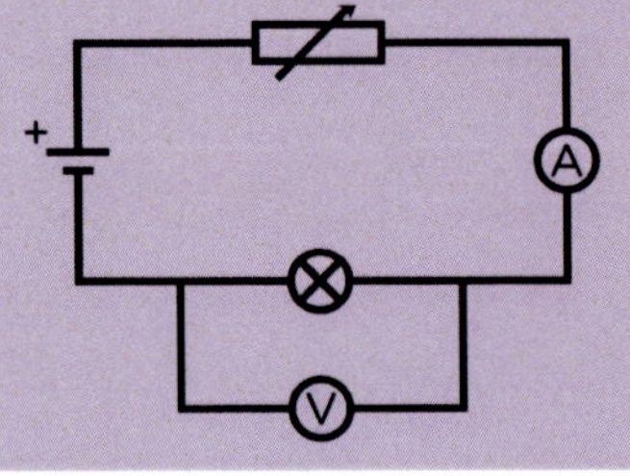

Types of resistors

- An ohmic conductor is one that has constant resistance. This means the current through the conductor is proportional to the potential difference across it.
  - Most wires and standard resistors behave as ohmic conductors, so long as their temperatures are kept constant.
  - Variable resistors are ohmic conductors that can have the value of their resistance manually changed.
- The resistance of a filament lamp increases as the current through it increases. This is because the current is causing the filament in the lamp to heat up.

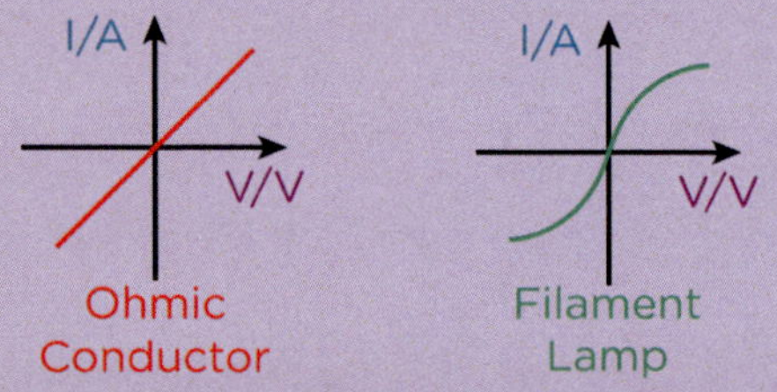

- A diode is a component that only allows current to flow in a single direction.
  - This is because its resistance is extremely high if the potential difference across it is below +0.7 V.
  - An LED is a diode that emits light when a current flows through it.

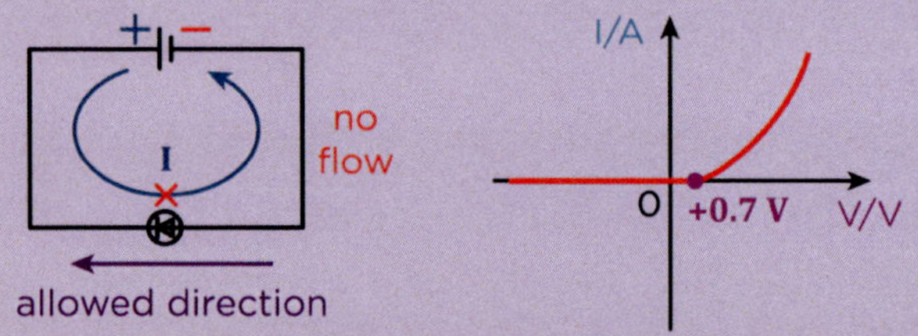

- The resistance of a thermistor decreases as its temperature increases. They can be used in circuits that react to temperature changes, such as thermostats.
- The resistance of an LDR decreases as the light intensity upon it increases. They can be used in circuits that react to changes in brightness in the surroundings, such as automatic lights.

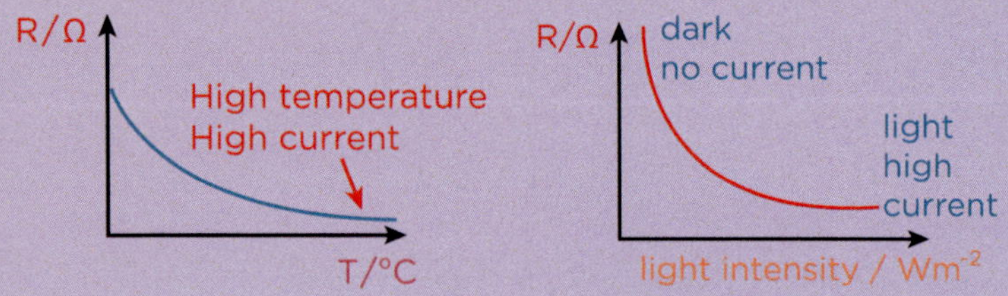

SNAPREVISE

Electrical power

- The power of an electrical appliance is given as power = potential difference × current. This can be written as $P = VI$ where:
  - P is the power of the appliance in W
  - V the potential difference across it in V
  - I is the current through it in A
- This can be combined with the resistance equation: power = $(\text{current})^2$ × resistance, or $P = I^2R$, where R is the resistance of the appliance in Ohms, Ω.
- Most household appliances have a power rating, which can be used to determine the current that should flow through it from mains electricity.

Electrical energy transfers

- Batteries and cells do work to move electrons around a circuit. This transfers the chemical energy in the battery to electrical energy in the circuit.
- Electrons will collide with atoms in a resistor, causing electrical energy to be transferred to thermal energy as the resistor becomes hot.
- The energy transferred by electrical work to a component is given as charge × potential difference. This can be written as $E = QV$ where:
  - E is the energy transferred in J
  - Q is the charge that flows through the component in C
  - V is the potential difference across the component in V
- The electrical energy transferred to an appliance is dependent on its power and the time it is turned on for. This is because energy transfer = power × time or $E = Pt$.
- Appliances will transfer energy from mains electricity or batteries to other forms.
  - Kettles will transfer energy to heat in water.
  - Motors will transfer energy to kinetic energy for rotation.

AC and DC currents

- A direct potential difference provides a direct current, which always flows in the same direction.
- An alternating potential difference causes an alternating current, which is constantly changing direction.
  - The number of times the current changes direction per second is its frequency.
  - Frequency is measured in Hertz, Hz, and 1 Hz is 1 cycle per second.
- In the UK, mains electricity is supplied as an AC current of ~230 V and 50 Hz.

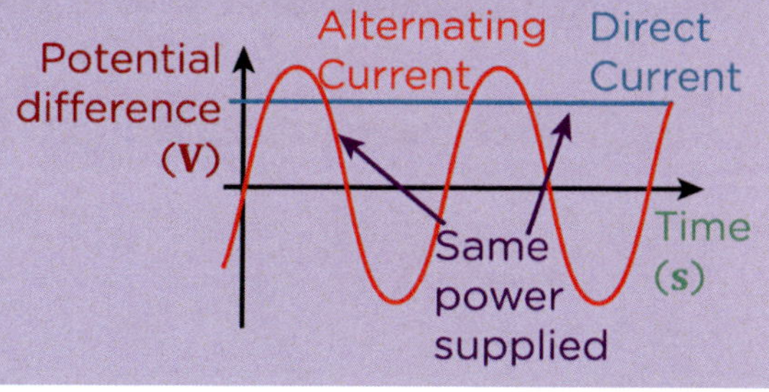

Three-core cables

- Most electrical appliances connect to a wall socket using cables containing three wires:
  - A live wire, which carries an alternating potential difference of 230 V from the mains supply.
  - A neutral wire, which completes the circuit and has a potential difference of close to 0 V.
  - The earth wire, which has a potential difference of 0 V. It is a safety wire which only carries current in case of a fault.

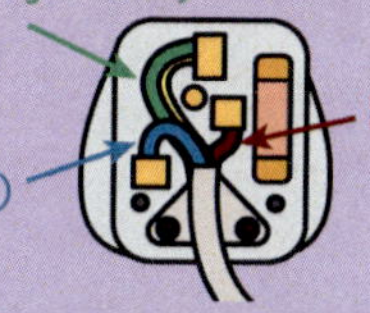

- There is a large potential difference between us and the live wire, so touching it would cause a current to flow through us and give us an electric shock.
- If the live wire touches a metallic appliance, then the earth wire is used to carry the resulting current away.

The National Grid

All specs except: *CIE, Pearson IGCSE, CCEA*

- The National Grid transfers electricity from power stations to consumers safely and efficiently.
  - Electricity is produced by generators in power stations at a high current.
  - Step-up transformers will raise the potential difference and lower the current.
  - This is transferred through long, overhead transmission cables. The low current means little energy is lost to heating in the cables.
  - A step-down transformer reduces the potential difference so it is suitable for domestic use.
- The transformers change potential difference using the equation:

$$\text{primary potential difference} \times \text{primary current} = \text{secondary potential difference} \times \text{secondary current}$$

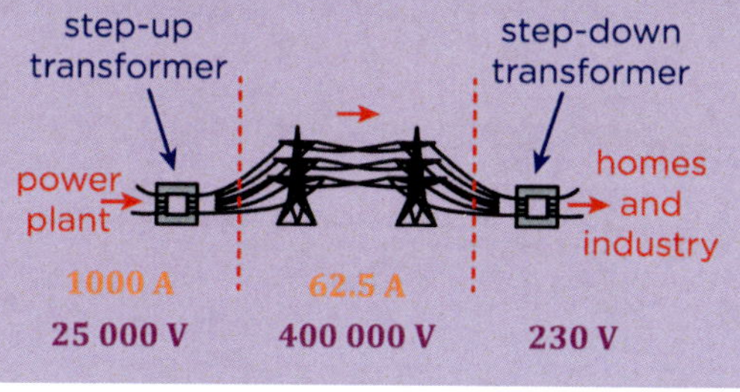

Volume and gases

Gas pressure and volume

- If the volume of a gas increases without changing its temperature, then the pressure it exerts will decrease.
  - This is because the particles hit the walls of the container at the same speed but less frequently because of the larger space.
  - The walls will also be larger, so the force per unit area (pressure) will also decrease.
- For a gas at a fixed temperature, $\text{pressure} \times \text{volume} = \text{constant}$. This can also be written as $pV = \text{const.}$ where:
  - p is the pressure of the gas in Pascals, Pa
  - V is its volume in m^3
  - const. is a constant value in Pa m^3, which won't change as p and V change.

Gas particles

- The particles in a gas move with random motion.
  - They travel in random directions with random speeds.
  - As the temperature of the gas increases, the particles gain more kinetic energy and their speeds increase.
- Gas particles will collide with each other and the walls of the container they are in.
  - No kinetic energy is lost during these collisions.
  - The collisions with the walls exert a force on them at right angles to them. This means the gas is exerting a pressure on the container.
  - Increasing the temperature of the gas without changing its volume increases this pressure, as the particles hit the walls with more force.

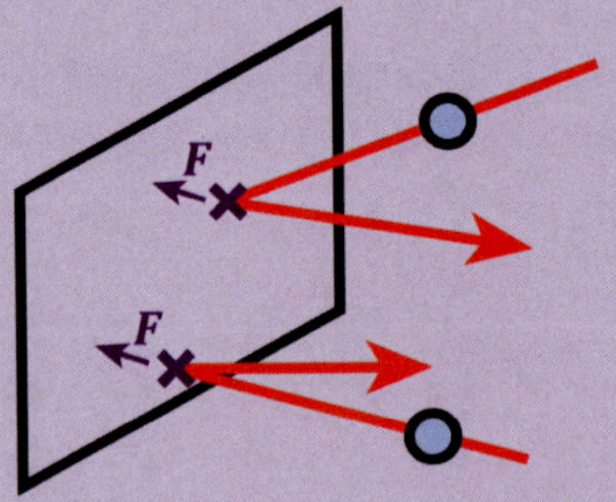

Work on gases

Higher tier

- Work is done on a gas when it is compressed or allowed to expand by applying a force (e.g. with a piston).
- Doing work on a gas increases its internal energy (the total kinetic and potential energy of particles).
- Compressing a gas leads to increased pressure and temperature if done quickly and energy isn't transferred away.
- The particles move faster when energy is transferred to the gas, increasing their kinetic energy. If a gas is compressed slowly, heat may be transferred to the surroundings, reducing temperature rise.
- Expanding a gas (e.g. allowing it to push a piston) causes the gas to do work on the surroundings, reducing internal energy.

Density

- The density of an object is given as $\text{density} = \text{mass} \div \text{volume}$ or $\rho = \frac{m}{V}$ where:
  - ρ is the density of an object in kg/m^3
  - m is its mass in kg
  - V is its volume in m^3
- Density is a property of a material. We say steel is heavier than plastic because steel has a higher density.
- Density is partially dependent on the atomic mass of the molecules making up a material.
- Determining the density of irregularly shaped objects requires measuring their volume. This can be done by placing them in a measuring cylinder filled with water and measuring the change in volume.

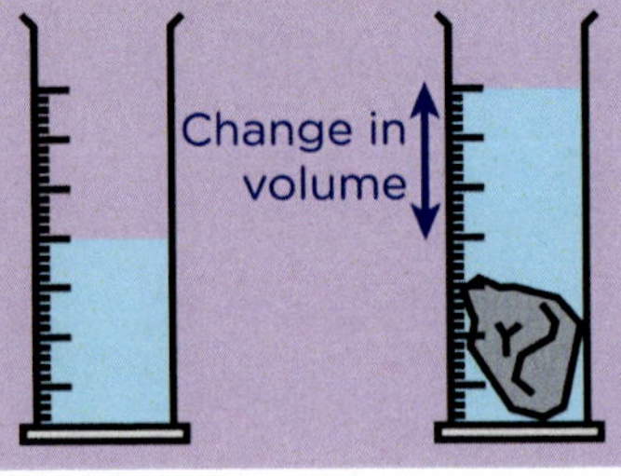

States of matter and heat capacity

SNAPREVISE

States of matter

- The different states of matter can be explained using particle models of atoms and molecules.
  - In a solid, the particles are all tightly packed in a rigid structure. They cannot move because of strong intermolecular forces but they can vibrate.
  - In a liquid, these forces are slightly weaker. The particles stay in contact but they can move and flow. The liquid can change shape to fit a container.
  - In a gas, the particles can freely move. They are spread out so the gas expands to fill any volume, and the forces between particles are very small.

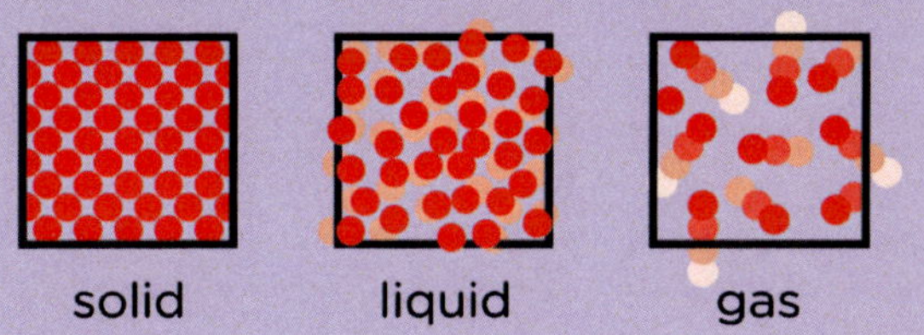

- Solids and liquids have high densities as atoms are tightly packed together. In gases, the density is much lower as the atoms or molecules are spread out.
- Substances can change state through various processes.
  - During these, mass is conserved as the number of particles doesn't change.
  - These are physical processes because they are reversible and the substance does not change.

Process	Change from...	To...
Melting	Solid	Liquid
Freezing	Liquid	Solid
Boiling/ evaporating	Liquid	Gas
Condensation	Gas	Liquid
Sublimation	Solid	Gas

Internal energy

- The internal energy of a system is the total kinetic and potential energy of the particles in the system.
- Internal energy represents the energy stored in a system.
- Heating a system will increase its internal energy in one of two ways:
  - The kinetic energy of the particles increases, causing them to move or vibrate faster. This raises the temperature of the system.
  - The potential energy increases due to a change of state. The substance will change from a solid to a liquid or from a liquid to a gas.

Specific heat capacity and latent heat

- The change in thermal energy associated with a temperature change in a system is given by $\text{energy} = \text{mass} \times \text{specific heat capacity} \times \text{temperature change}$ or $\Delta E = mc\Delta\theta$.
- When heating a substance as it is changing state, its internal energy will increase but its temperature will not change. This can be noticed on a heating or cooling graph for the substance.
- The specific latent heat of a substance is the energy required to change the state of one kilogram of the substance without changing its temperature.
  - The specific latent heat of fusion is the specific latent heat for changing the substance from solid to liquid.
  - The specific latent heat of vaporisation is the specific latent heat for changing the substance from liquid to gas.
- The energy required to change state is given by $\text{energy} = \text{mass} \times \text{specific latent heat}$. This can be written as $E = mL$ where:
  - E is the energy required to change state in J
  - m is the mass of the substance in kg
  - L is its specific latent heat in J/kg

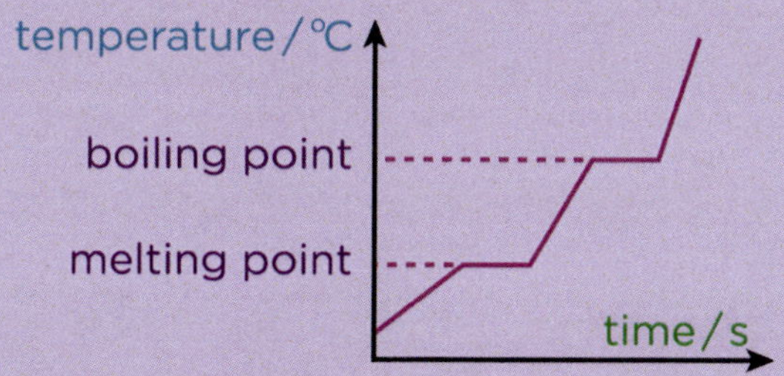

SNAPREVISE

Structure of the atom

- Materials are made up of atoms, which have a radius of around 1×10^{10} m.
- Each atom contains a nucleus, consisting of positively charged protons and uncharged neutrons.
  - The nucleus is around 1/10,000 the size of the atom.
  - Almost all the atom's mass is contained in the nucleus.
- The nucleus is surrounded by negatively charged electrons.
  - These electrons move in set energy levels at different distances from the nucleus.
  - An electron will move further from the nucleus and increase its energy level by absorbing electromagnetic radiation.
  - It will move towards the nucleus and decrease its energy level by emitting electromagnetic radiation.

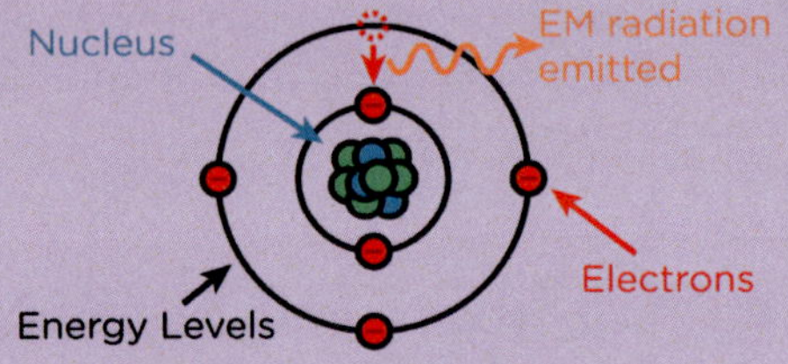

Atomic notation

- Atoms are represented using atomic notation, e.g. $^{56}_{26}Fe$ where:
  - 56 is the mass number, which is equal to the total number of protons and neutrons in the nucleus.
  - 26 is the atomic number, equal to the number of protons in the nucleus.
  - Fe is the element the atom is of. This is determined by the atomic number.
- The number of neutrons in a nucleus is given by $\text{mass number} - \text{atomic number}$.

Ions and isotopes

- The number of protons in an atom is equal to the number of electrons it has.
  - Protons have equal and opposite charges to electrons.
  - So, the atom has no overall charge.
- Ions are particles that have charge due to an imbalance in proton and electron numbers.
  - Removing electrons from an atom will result in a positively charged ion.
  - Adding electrons to an atom will result in a negatively charged ion.
- Isotopes are atoms of the same element but with different masses. They will have the same number of protons and electrons but different numbers of neutrons.

$^{4}_{2}He^{-}$ (ion) $^{4}_{2}He$ $^{3}_{2}He$ (isotope)

Development of atomic models

All specs except: WJEC, CIE, Pearson IGCSE

- The idea of an atom as a tiny sphere that could not be divided was first suggested by Democritus in ancient Greece. This idea has evolved over time with new evidence.
- The discovery of the electron led J. J. Thomson to suggest the "plum pudding" model of the atom in 1904:
  - The atom consists of a sphere of positive charge that is evenly spread throughout.
  - Negatively charged electrons are dotted around this sphere.

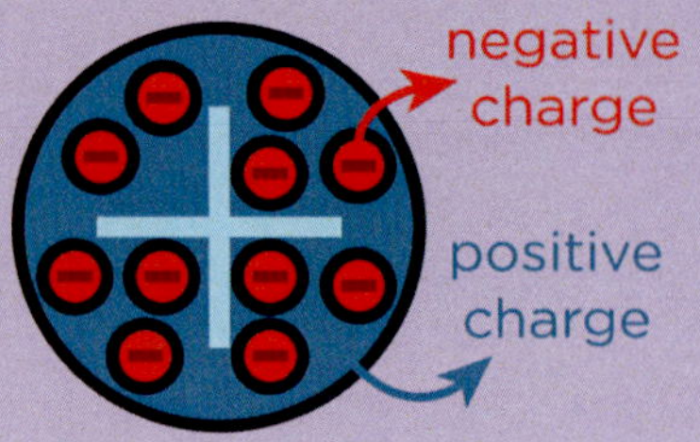

- Geiger and Marsden's alpha scattering experiment led to Rutherford suggesting the nuclear model of the atom in 1911:
  - Alpha particles were fired at a thin sheet of gold foil. The plum pudding model suggested the alpha particles would pass straight through the foil.
  - Instead, a small number experience slight deflections with an even smaller number experiencing heavy deflections.
  - The nuclear model of the atom suggests the atom consists of mostly empty space. Almost all the mass and all the positive charge of the atom is contained in a very small nucleus.

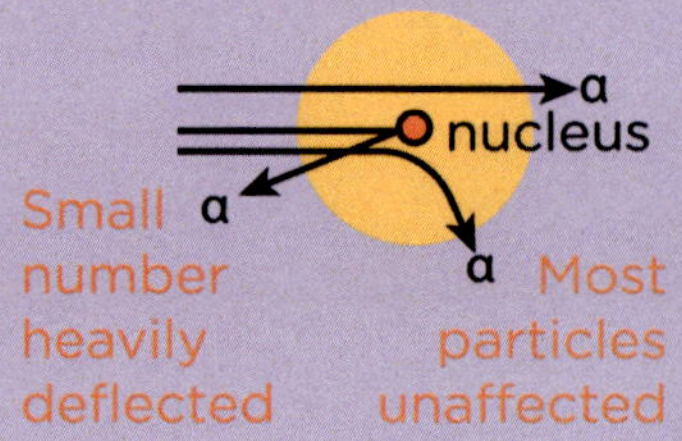

- Later experiments led to the conclusion that the positive charge of the nucleus could be subdivided into smaller particles called protons.
- Niels Bohr adapted the nuclear model in 1913 to explain the role of electrons in the atom:
  - Electrons orbit the nucleus in set energy levels. These electrons emit or absorb electromagnetic radiation to change levels.
  - Bohr's theoretical calculations around these energy levels were later supported by experimental observations.
- In 1932, James Chadwick discovered that the nucleus also contained uncharged neutrons, which contribute to its mass.

Properties of radiation and ionisation

- Certain nuclei are unstable, meaning they will undergo radioactive decay and emit radiation to become more stable.
- This radiation can ionise atoms, causing them to become ions.
- Activity is the rate of radioactive decay, measured in Becquerels (emissions per second).
- Detectors, such as a Geiger-Muller tube, can measure radioactivity by counting the number of particles entering it. This will give a count rate as the number of decays recorded per second.
- Nuclear radiation comes in multiple forms:
  - Alpha particles (α) consisting of two protons and two neutrons released from the nucleus (the same as a helium nucleus).
  - Beta particles (β) consisting of a high-speed electron. A neutron will turn into a proton to release this.
  - Gamma rays (γ) consisting of electromagnetic radiation from the nucleus.
  - A neutron (n) released from the nucleus.

Radiation	Range in Air	Stopped by	Ionising power
Alpha	5 cm	Paper	Strong
Beta	Several metres	Aluminium sheet	Medium
Gamma	Near infinite	Thick lead	Weak

- Radiation is harmful to the body as it can damage cells and tissues.
  - Alpha radiation is the most damaging inside the body as it is the most ionising.
  - Gamma radiation is the most damaging outside the body as it can penetrate the body from far away.

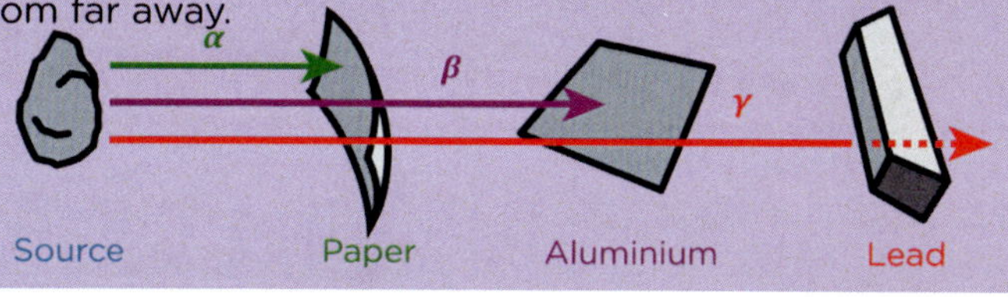

Nuclear equations

- An alpha particle can be denoted as $^{4}_{2}He$.
  - Alpha decay will cause the atomic number of a nucleus to decrease by 2 and its mass number to decrease by 4. For example, $^{235}_{92}U \rightarrow ^{231}_{90}Th + ^{4}_{2}He$.
- A beta particle can be denoted as $^{0}_{-1}e$.
  - Beta decay will cause the atomic number of a nucleus to increase by 1 while keeping its mass number the same. For example, $^{99}_{43}Tc \rightarrow ^{99}_{44}Ru + ^{0}_{-1}e$.
- Gamma rays are emitted after alpha or beta decays to carry away excess energy the nucleus has. This does not affect the mass or atomic number of the nucleus.

Half-lives

- Radioactive decay is a random process, meaning it is impossible to predict which nuclei in a radioactive sample will decay next or when.
  - Radioactive decay is unaffected by external physical conditions, such as temperature. Each nucleus has an equal chance of being the next to decay.
  - For a large number of radioactive nuclei, it can be calculated what proportion of nuclei will decay in a period of time.
- The half-life, $t_{1/2}$, of a radioactive isotope is the time it takes half the nuclei in a sample of that isotope to decay.
  - This will also be the time it takes the activity of the sample to halve.
  - Half-life will be the same for any sized sample and throughout its decay.
  - After n half-lives, the number of undecayed nuclei will be $\frac{1}{2^n}$ of its initial value.
- Half-life is a property determined by the isotope of a nucleus. The shorter the half-life, the faster an isotope will decay.

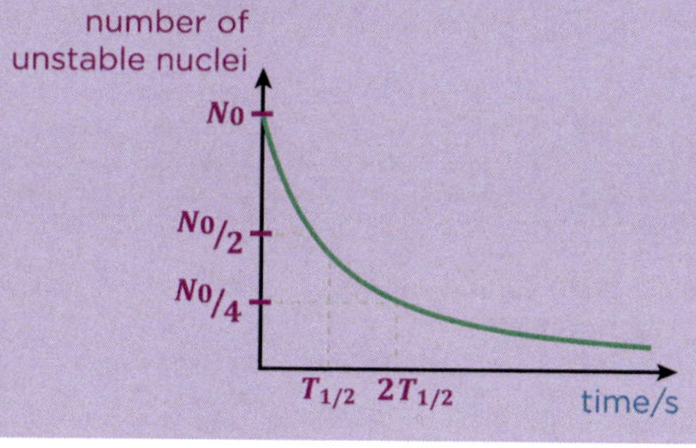

Contamination and irradiation

- Contamination is when radioactive materials are present where they are unwanted.
  - This poses a hazard as these materials will irradiate their surroundings, potentially without anyone realising this is happening.
  - Contamination can be caused by mishandling of radioactive materials or damage to nuclear power stations.
- Irradiation is the process of exposing an object to radiation.
  - This poses a hazard due to the potential damage the radiation can do to the body.
  - Irradiation can be useful in small, controlled doses.
  - Irradiation does not cause contamination.
  - Irradiation can be caused by unsafe handling of radioactive materials or exposure to contaminated materials.

Nuclear fusion and fission

Background radiation and dose

All specs except: OCR A, OCR B

- There is always a small amount of background radiation around us due to:
  - Radon gas in the atmosphere and cosmic rays from space.
  - Small amounts of radioactive isotopes in rocks and building materials.
  - Man-made sources, such as nuclear power stations and weapons.
- When measuring activity, a background count should be taken to distinguish the activity from a sample from background radiation.
- The radiation dose a person receives is measured in sieverts, Sv.
  - A dose of 10 mSv or lower will not cause immediate harm but could increase the risk of cancer.
  - A dose of 1,000 mSv will not be fatal but can make people unwell for some time.
  - A dose of around 4,000 mSv will be fatal.
- Background radiation alone will give extremely small doses. The exact dose a person receives will depend on location and occupation.

Uses of radiation

- The hazards and uses associated with radioactive isotopes depend on their half-lives:
  - Short half-lives mean isotopes are dangerous for a short period of time but are safe in the long term.
  - Long half-lives mean isotopes cause little irradiation but could cause damage through long-term exposure.
- Radioactive isotopes can be used as radioactive tracers.
  - Technetium-99 or another radioactive liquid is injected into the body and absorbed by an organ or system. The radiation it emits is detected outside the body.
  - Gamma emitters should be used as they cause minimal damage from inside the body. They should also have short half-lives so they can be detected but don't cause long-term damage.
- Radiation can be used in cancer treatment:
  - Intense gamma radiation can be directed at a tumour from outside the body to kill cancerous cells.
  - An alpha or beta emitter can be injected into the body to supply radiation directly to the tumour.

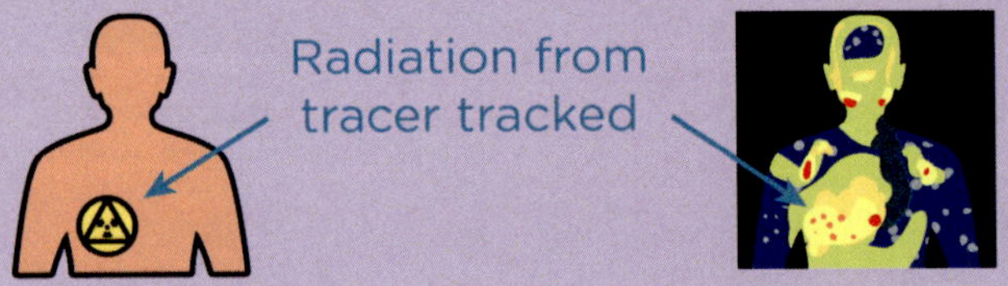

Nuclear fission

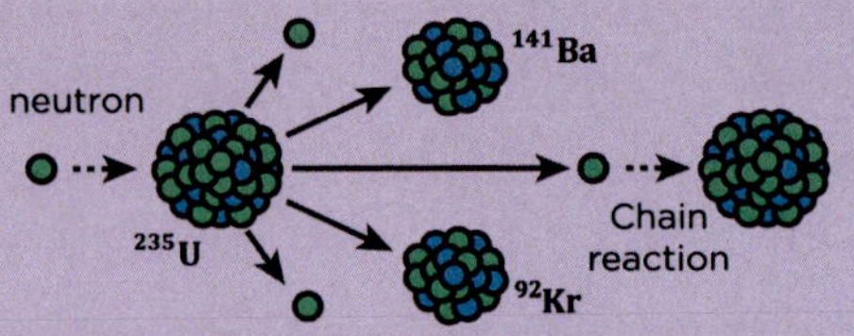

- Nuclear fission is the process of a large, unstable nucleus splitting into two smaller nuclei. These two nuclei are similar in size but rarely identical.
- Gamma rays will also be released after the fission reaction, along with 2 or 3 neutrons.
- Fission rarely happens spontaneously. It is typically induced by a neutron colliding with the unstable nucleus. The neutrons released in the fission reaction can then collide with other unstable nuclei to cause a chain reaction.
- A large amount of energy is released in the reaction:
  - The smaller nuclei gain kinetic energy due to their electrostatic repulsion.
  - This energy is transferred to the internal energy of atoms the nuclei collide with, raising the temperature of the system.

Nuclear reactors

- A nuclear reactor harnesses the energy released by fission:
  - Fuel rods of uranium-238 and uranium-235 are lowered into a reactor. Neutrons released from one rod cause a fission reaction of uranium-235 in another.
  - Control rods made of boron absorb neutrons released during fission to control the rate of chain reactions. The further the rods are lowered the slower the rate will be.
  - A thick concrete shield prevents neutrons and other radiation from escaping the reactor.
- Failing to control the chain reaction will cause energy to be released at an extremely fast rate. This is the principle used in a nuclear bomb.

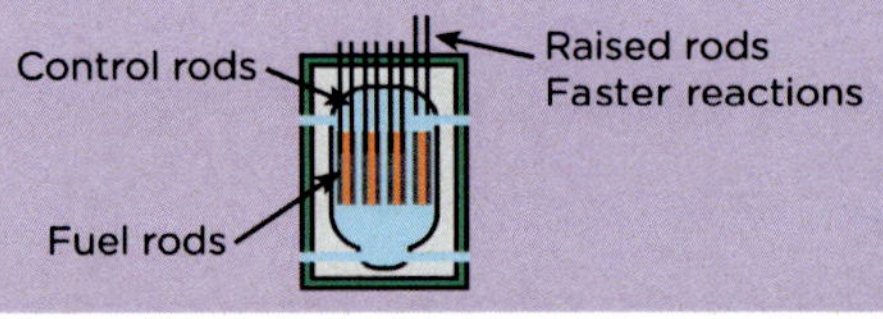

Nuclear fusion

- Nuclear fusion is the process of joining together two small nuclei into a larger nucleus.
- This is extremely difficult to achieve but happens continuously in stars.
- The fusion reaction causes a large amount of energy to be released. This is what causes the star to be hot and bright.

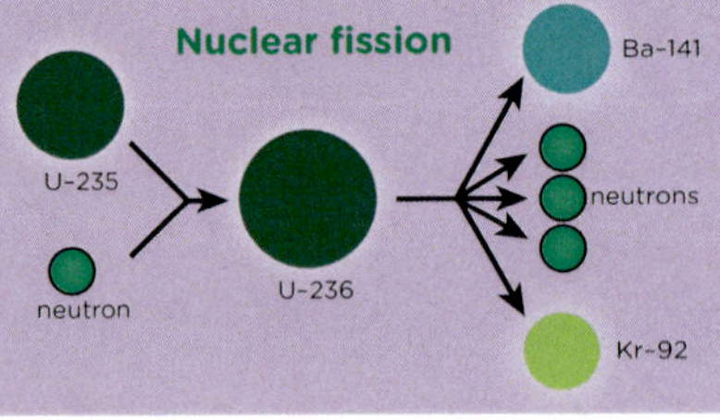

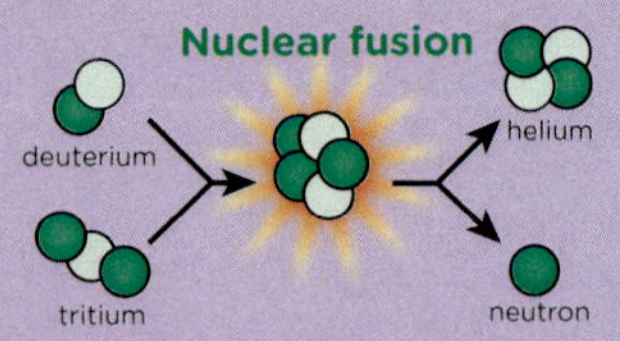

Forces

SNAPREVISE

Defining forces

- A force is a push or pull that one object performs on another, which can change the direction an object is moving in, change the speed of an object, or deform an object and change its shape.
- Contact forces act between objects that are physically touching. Non-contact forces act between objects that are physically separated.
- A force is a vector quantity that is measured in Newtons, N.

	Force	Description
Contact forces	Friction	Force a surface performs on an object moving along it to try and stop it.
Contact forces	Air resistance	Force that acts on an object moving through air to slow it down.
Contact forces	Drag	Force a fluid performs on an object moving through it to try and slow it down. Air resistance is a form of drag that acts on objects moving through air.
Contact forces	Tension	Force a rope exerts on an object when it is pulled.
Contact forces	Normal contact force	Force caused by a surface pushing against an object in contact with it.
Non-contact forces	Gravitational force	Force that causes Earth to pull objects downwards and the Sun to keep planets in orbit.
Non-contact forces	Electrostatic force	Force that causes charged objects to attract/repel each other.
Non-contact forces	Magnetic	Force that pulls magnetic materials (e.g. iron, steel) towards magnets.

Resultant force

- A resultant force is a single force that has the same effect on an object as the multiple forces acting on it.
- If two forces are acting in the same direction, then the resultant will be the sum in that direction.
- If they are acting in opposite directions, then the resultant will be their difference in the direction of the larger force.

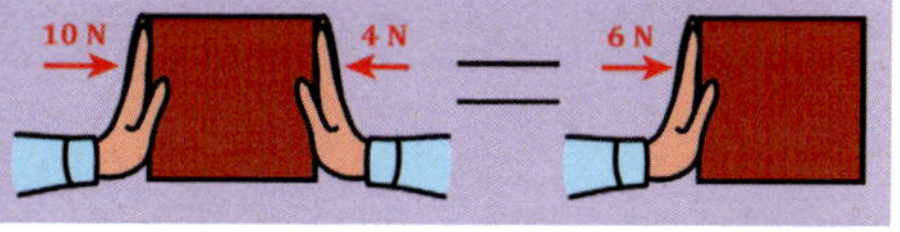

Free body diagrams

- A free body diagram shows the forces acting on an object with arrows to signify the forces and their directions.
- The resultant force in the horizontal and vertical directions can be found by finding then adding or subtracting the forces in those directions.

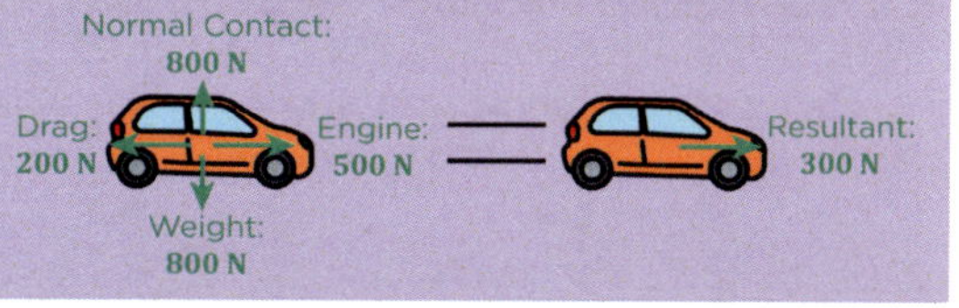

Scalars and vectors

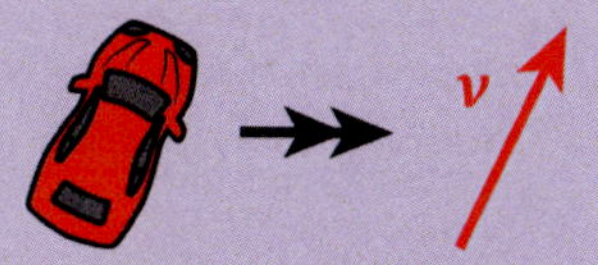

- Quantities can be scalars or vectors. **Scalars** only have size, whereas **vectors** have both size and direction.
- Vector quantities can be represented as arrows that point in the direction of the vector. Their length represents the size of the vector.
- **Distance** is a scalar quantity that describes how far an object moves or how far apart two objects are. **Displacement** is a vector quantity measured as a straight line from a start point to a finish point.

Resolving forces

Higher tier

- Resolving a force is the process of splitting a force into two perpendicular components. The resultant of these two components will be the original force.
  - Draw the original force as a vector arrow in the correct direction and to a suitable scale.
  - Draw a horizontal line from the start of the vector to a point that lines up vertically with its end.
  - Draw a vertical line from this point to the end of the vector.
  - Measure the lengths of the horizontal and vertical lines to determine the size of these components.

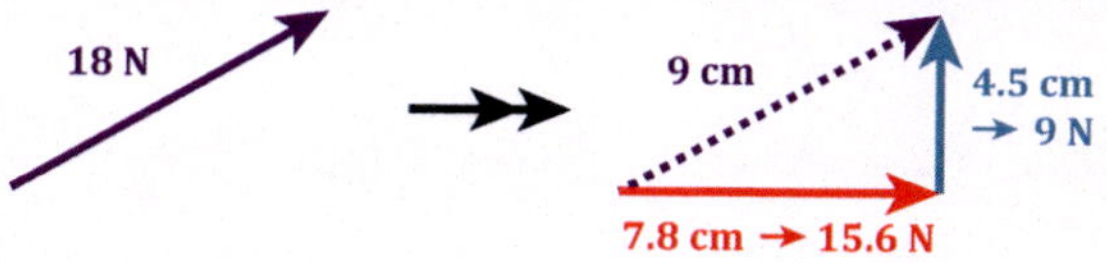

Work done and energy transfer from work

- A force does work on an object when it causes the object to move. The work done by a force is given by work = force × distance moved (in the direction of the force) .
- This can be written as $W = Fs$ where W is the work done in J, F is the magnitude of the force doing the work in N, and s is the distance the force causes an object to move in m. This equation assumes the object is moving in the direction of the force. No work is done if the object is stationary or the force is perpendicular to the direction the object is moving in.
- Work is measured in joules, J. One joule is the work done by a 1 N force to move an object 1 m. The units joules and Newton-metres, Nm, are the same.

- An energy transfer will occur when a force does work. This is why work and energy have the same unit. For instance, lifting an object will cause work to be transferred to gravitational potential energy. Holding a heavy object stationary will cause you to get tired as your muscles transfer energy, but they do no work.
- Pushing or pulling an object will cause work to be transferred to kinetic energy.
- If you are doing work against friction, then this work will be transferred to thermal energy in the object. This is why objects heat up when we rub them together.

Velocity and acceleration

SNAPREVISE

Speed and velocity

- Speed is a scalar quantity that describes how fast an object is moving (or increasing the distance it has travelled).
- The constant speed and the distance travelled by an object are related by the equation $\text{distance travelled} = \text{speed} \times \text{time}$. This equation can also be used to calculate the average speed of a complete journey.
- Velocity is a vector quantity, given as an object's speed in a particular direction.
- Few objects move at a constant speed. They will have small variations in speed during their motion. This also applies to sound waves and wind.
- The average speed at which people travel by walking, running or cycling is affected by numerous factors, including their age and fitness, how far they are travelling, and the terrain they are travelling on.

Motion	Typical speed
Walking	1.5 m/s
Running	3 m/s
Cycling	6 m/s
Car (on a motorway)	30 m/s
Train	60 m/s
Jet plane	200 m/s
Sound wave	330 m/s

Acceleration

- Acceleration is the rate at which an object's speed is changing.
- An object that is speeding up is accelerating. An object that is slowing down is decelerating.
- The average acceleration of an object is given by the equation $\text{acceleration} = \text{change in velocity} \div \text{time}$. This can be written as $a = \frac{\Delta v}{t}$ where:
  - a is the average acceleration in m/s^2
  - Δv is the change in velocity in m/s, and t is the time in s.

Uniform acceleration equation

- For an object that has constant acceleration, the following equation holds: $(\text{final velocity})^2 - (\text{initial velocity})^2 = 2 \times \text{acceleration} \times \text{distance travelled}$. This can be written as $v^2 - u^2 = 2as$ where:
  - v is the final velocity in m/s
  - u is the initial velocity in m/s
  - a is the constant acceleration in m/s^2
  - s is the distance travelled in m.

Distance–time graphs

- A distance-time graph shows how the distance travelled by an object changes with time.
- The speed of the object can be found by calculating the gradient of the graph.
  - A steeper gradient means a greater speed.
  - If the graph is horizontal, then the object is not moving.
- The distance-time graph for an accelerating object will be curved. The speed at a point in time can be found by measuring the gradient of the tangent to the graph at that point.

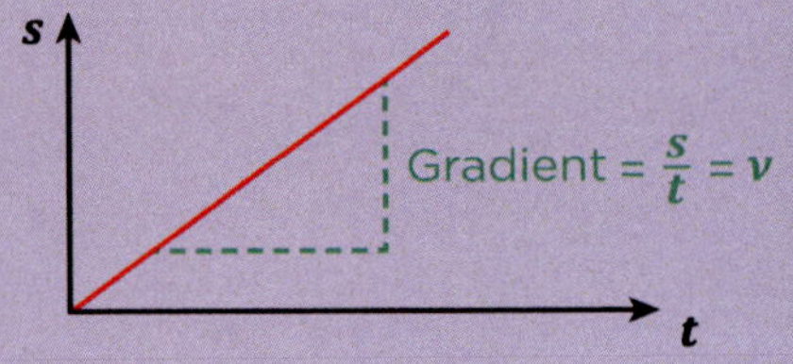

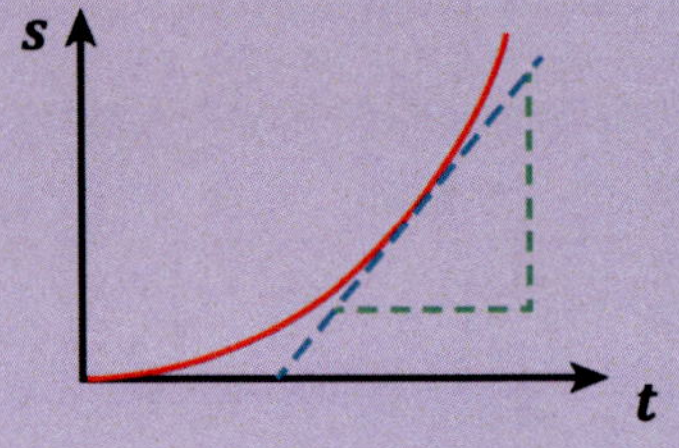

Velocity–time graphs

Higher tier

- A velocity-time graph shows how the velocity of an object changes with time.
- The acceleration of the object can be found by calculating the gradient of the graph.
  - A steeper gradient means a greater acceleration.
  - If the graph is horizontal, then the object is moving at a constant velocity.
- The area under a velocity-time graph gives the distance travelled by an object.
  - For straight graphs, this can be calculated as the area of multiple triangles and rectangles.
  - For curved graphs, this distance can be estimated by counting the squares under the graph.

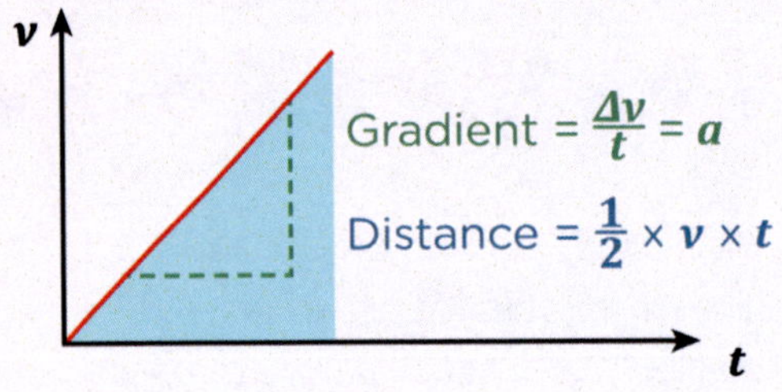

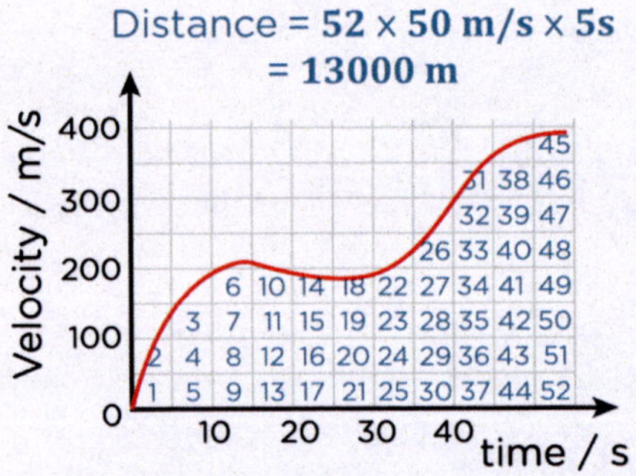

The distance each square represents is the velocity its height represents multiplied by the time its width represents

Gravity and calculating weight

- Large objects, such as the Earth, will produce a **gravitational field**. Masses inside the gravitational field will experience a force called **weight**.
- Weight will pull the mass towards the centre of the field. On Earth, this will pull masses down toward its surface.
- Weight will act through a single point in the object called its **centre of mass.** Smaller objects also produce gravitational fields, but the forces from these are too small to be noticed.

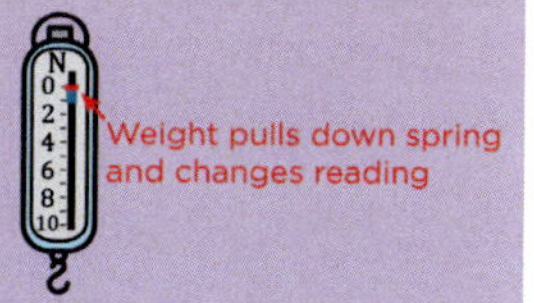

- The weight of an object can be measured using a spring balance.
- The weight an object experiences depends on its **mass** and **gravitational field strength**, given by $\text{weight} = \text{mass} \times \text{gravitational field strength}$ or $W = mg$.
    - Mass is how much matter makes up an object. An object's mass will be the same in any gravitational field at any point in the universe.
    - **Gravitational field strength** is the force a 1 kg object would experience at a point in a gravitational field, given in N/kg. This will depend on location in the field and what is producing the field.
    - On the Earth's surface, the gravitational field strength has a constant value of **9.8 N/kg.** This means that on Earth, **mass is proportional to weight.** However, on other planets, the weight of an object will change while its mass will not.

Acceleration due to gravity and terminal velocity

- Any object that is falling, with the only force affecting it being gravity, will have an acceleration of 9.8 m/s^2.
- When an object is falling through a fluid, it will initially accelerate downwards because of gravity. This motion will cause **air resistance** or **drag forces** to affect it. Eventually, the drag forces will equal the gravitational force and the object will stop accelerating. The constant speed it now travels at is its **terminal velocity**.
- The terminal velocity and the time it takes to reach it can be decreased by increasing the surface area of the object, such as by using a parachute, or increasing the thickness of the fluid, such as by falling in water rather than air.

- For example, as a parachutist falls through the air:
    - Their downward velocity will first increase rapidly due to acceleration by gravity.
    - As air resistance starts to affect them, this acceleration will start to decrease. However, their velocity is still increasing as their weight is greater than drag forces.
    - The air resistance will increase with their speed, to a point where it is equal to their weight. The parachutist now falls at a constant terminal velocity.
    - When the parachutist opens the parachute, the increase in surface area causes a sudden increase in air resistance and decelerates.
    - Eventually, air resistance decreases to match weight again, and the parachutist falls at a slower terminal velocity.

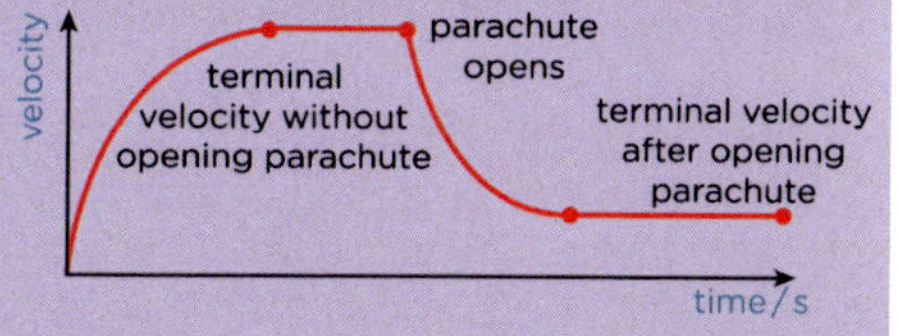

Circular motion

Higher tier

- When an object travels in a circle:
    - It is travelling at a constant speed.
    - The direction it is travelling in is constantly changing.
    - As a result, its velocity is constantly changing.
- Examples of objects that travel in circles are satellites in orbit, cars travelling around bends, planes banking to change direction, and fairground rides, such as Ferris Wheels.

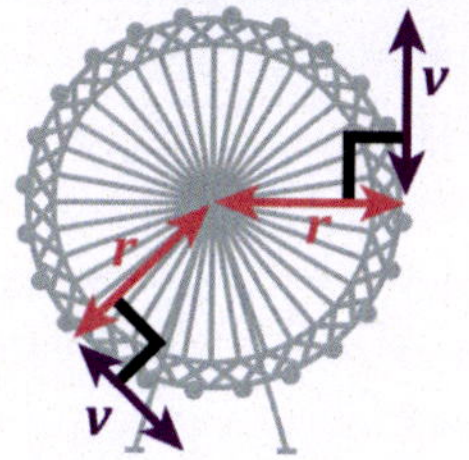

Newton's First Law

- Newton's first law states that **if the resultant force on an object is zero then it will experience no acceleration**. This means the object will either:
    - Remain stationary.
    - Travel at the same, constant velocity.
- **Inertia** is the tendency of an object to remain at rest or continue moving with uniform motion.

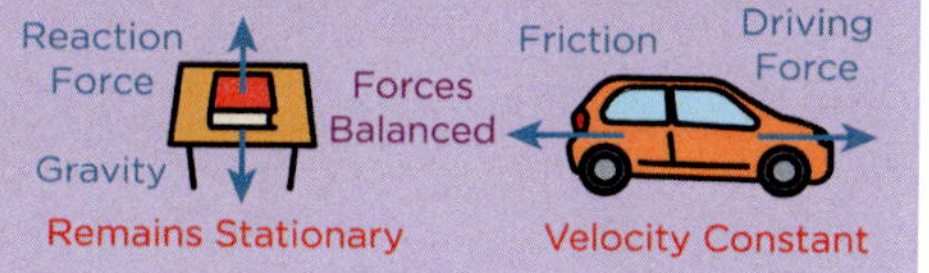

Newton's Second Law

- Newton's second law states that the **acceleration of an object is proportional to the resultant force** acting on it and **inversely proportional to its mass.**
- This law can be written as the equation $\text{resultant force} = \text{mass} \times \text{acceleration}$. This can also be written as $F = ma$ where F is the resultant force in N, m is the mass in kg, and a is the acceleration in m/s^2.
- The **inertial mass** of an object is a measure of how difficult it is to change an object's velocity. It can be calculated as $\text{inertial mass} = \text{force} \div \text{acceleration}$ or $m = \frac{F}{a}$.

Newton's Third Law

- Newton's third law states that **if an object exerts a force on another object, that object will exert an equal and opposite force**, of the same type, on the first.
- Examples of Newton's third law in action:
    - When an object is pulled towards Earth by gravity, the object is also pulling the Earth towards it.
    - When two charges repel or attract, they both experience the same force towards or away from each other.
    - When you stand on a floor, the floor exerts an upward reaction force that is equal to your weight pushing down on it.

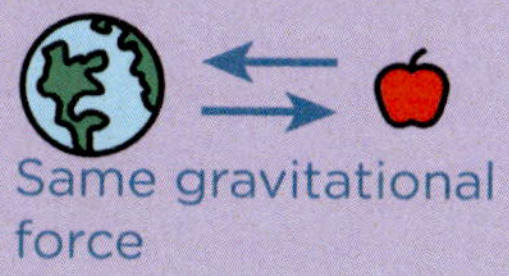

Moments

- The **moment** of a force is the **turning effect** it causes.
- The moment can be calculated as $\text{moment} = \text{force} \times \text{distance}$ or $M = Fd$ where:
  - M is the moment of the force in Nm,
  - F is the force in N
  - d is the perpendicular distance from the line the force acts on to the pivot of the object it is acting on in m
- **Levers** help to improve the moment from a force by allowing it to act far from a pivot. They are used to lift heavy objects that are close to the pivot and so the moment of their weight is small.
- **Gears** will exert contact forces on each other of equal magnitude. The radius of the gear determines the turning effect this force produces.

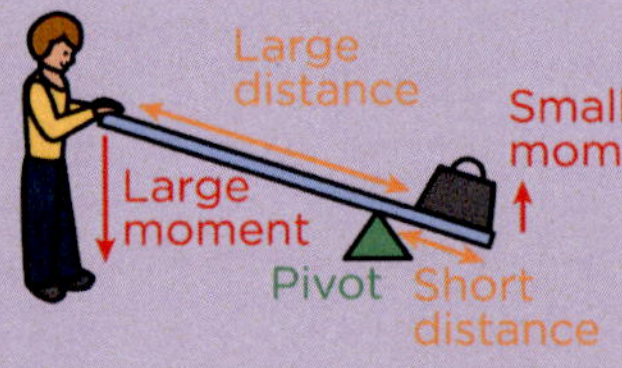

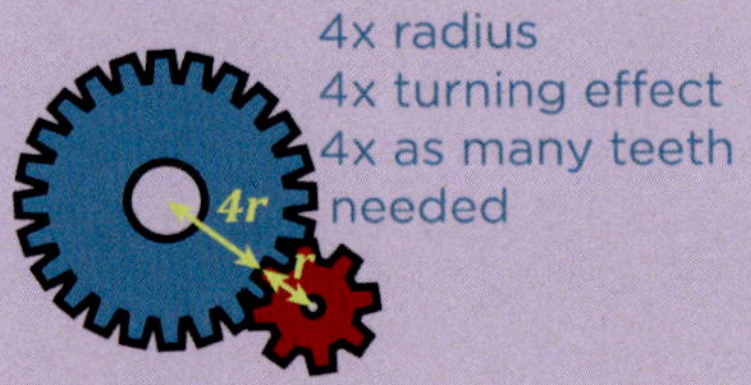

Resultant moment

- Moments can be directed **clockwise** or **anticlockwise** about a pivot.
  - The resultant moment is the difference between the total clockwise and anticlockwise moment. An object will turn in the direction of the resultant moment.
  - If the resultant moment is zero (meaning the clockwise and anticlockwise moments are equal) then the object doesn't turn and is in equilibrium. This is the principle of moments.
- Cranes and other machinery that could topple use **counterweights** to balance the moment from their load.

Deformation

- A single force will only cause a stationary object to move. To **deform** (change the shape of) an object, **multiple forces** must be used:
  - Two forces pulling in opposite directions can stretch an object.
  - Two forces pushing in opposite directions can compress an object.
  - Two forces pushing in one direction at the ends of an object and one pushing in its centre can bend it.

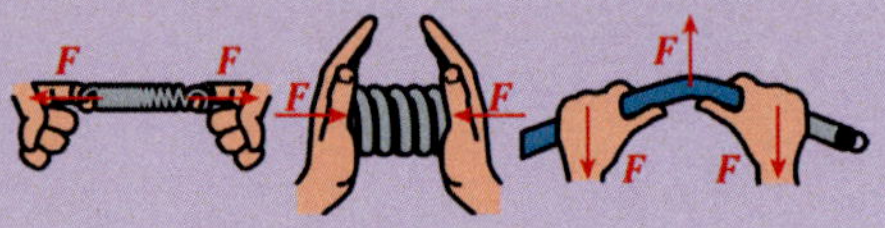

- Stretches can be **elastic** or **inelastic**:
  - An object will return to its original length after an elastic deformation.
  - An object will be permanently stretched after an inelastic deformation.

Extending springs

- The force required to stretch a spring is given by $\text{force} = \text{spring constant} \times \text{extension}$.
- The **spring constant,** or **stiffness** of a spring, determines how difficult it is to stretch. It is the force required to stretch the spring by 1 m, given in N/m. This equation can also be written as $F = ke$ where:
  - F is the force causing the extension in N
  - k is the spring constant in N/m
  - e is the extension in m
- This equation can also be applied when e instead represents the distance the spring has been compressed.
- This equation will only apply to springs that have not been stretched beyond their **limit of proportionality.**
  - This is the extension after which force is no longer proportional to extension.
  - Inelastic deformation starts after this point.

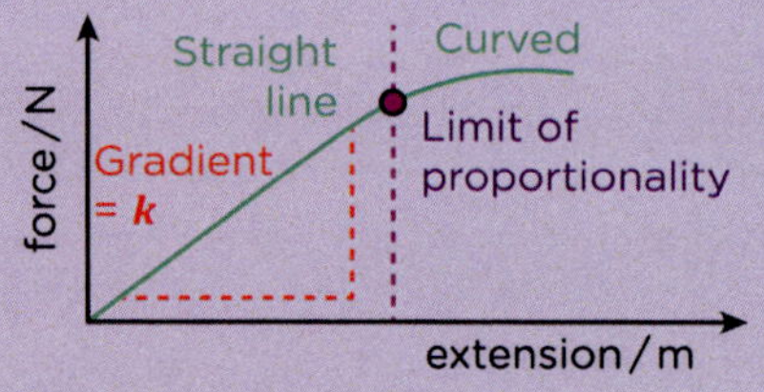

Elastic potential energy

- The work done to stretch a spring means energy is stored in a spring as elastic potential energy, given by $\text{elastic potential energy} = \frac{1}{2} \times \text{spring constant} \times (\text{extension})^2$ or $F = \frac{1}{2}ke^2$.
- No energy is stored in objects that deform inelastically. Instead, the work done on them causes them to heat up.

SNAPREVISE

Fluid pressure

All specs except: WJEC

- A fluid is a substance that can flow, it is a liquid or a gas.
- Fluid in a container will exert a force on the walls of the container, at right angles to each wall.
- The pressure a force exerts on a surface is given by the equation pressure = force normal to a surface ÷ area of the surface or $p = \frac{F}{a}$ where:
  - p is the pressure in pascals, Pa
  - F is the force normal to a surface in N
  - A is the area of the surface in m^2

Column pressure

All specs except: WJEC, CIE

- As an object falls to a lower depth in a liquid, the pressure the liquid exerts on it increases. This is because there is a greater weight of liquid above the object.
- The pressure an object experiences at the bottom of a column of water is given by pressure = height of column × density of liquid × gravitational field strength. This can be written as $p = h\rho g$ where:
  - p is the pressure in Pa
  - h is the height of the column in m
  - ρ is the density of the liquid in kg/m^3
  - g is the gravitational field strength in N/kg

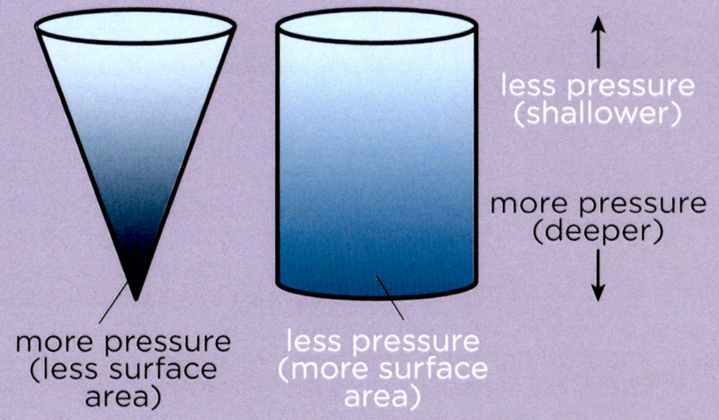

Upthrust

Only: AQA, OCR A, OCR B

- The pressure on the bottom surface of a submerged object will be greater than the pressure on the top surface. This pressure difference results in a force called upthrust.
- This upthrust will try to push the object upwards to the surface of the liquid.
- The size of the upthrust force is equal to the weight of the fluid that has been displaced by the object.
- An object will float if the upthrust force is greater than its weight.
  - Objects with densities greater than that of the liquid will sink.
  - Objects with densities less than that of the liquid will float on the liquid's surface, partially submerged. How much of the object is submerged depends on how dense it is compared to the liquid.

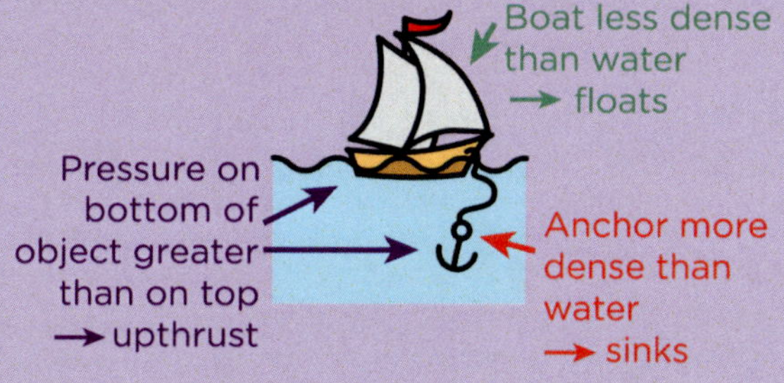

Atmospheric pressure

All specs except: WJEC, CIE

- Air particles are pulled towards the Earth by its gravitational field. This forms a layer of air around the Earth called the atmosphere.
- Atmospheric pressure is the pressure air molecules exert on a surface as they collide with it.
- Atmospheric pressure decreases with height above the Earth's surface.
  - This is because the air density decreases, and so there are fewer air molecules.
  - This means collisions between air molecules and surfaces happen less frequently, so the force exerted by the molecules is smaller.

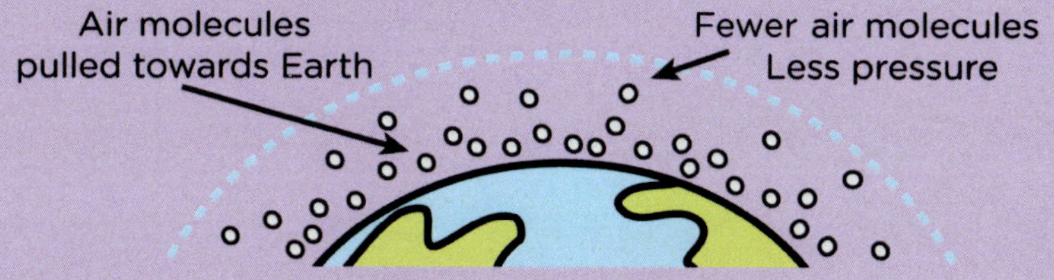

Stopping, braking, and momentum

SNAPREVISE

Stopping distance and reaction time

All specs except: CIE, CCEA

- The stopping distance of a vehicle is the distance it will travel before decelerating to a stop. It is the **sum of the thinking distance and braking distance.**
  - The thinking distance will be the distance travelled before the driver reacts to the need to stop. Thinking distance is changed by conditions affecting the driver while braking distance is affected by conditions affecting the vehicle or road.
  - The braking distance will be the distance the vehicle travels after its brakes are applied. The braking distance of a vehicle will increase if:
    - The roads are slippery, icy, smooth or other conditions that will reduce the friction it causes.
    - The braking force the vehicle can provide is reduced.
    - The vehicle is not maintained well, particularly its tyres and brakes.
- The greater the speed of a vehicle, the further its stopping distance will be.
- People's reaction times will vary. They are typically between 0.2 s and 0.9 s.
- Reaction times can be tested by asking someone to grab a ruler as it is dropped or press a timed button after a light comes on.
- A driver's reaction time will be increased by drinking alcohol, drugs and certain medications, tiredness, or becoming distracted (e.g. using a phone whilst driving).

Estimating stopping distance

All specs except: CIE, CCEA

- Average stopping distances for cars at varying speeds are given in the UK Highway Code:
  - A car travelling at 20 mph will have a thinking distance of around 6 m and a braking distance of around 6 m.
  - A car travelling at 70 mph will have a thinking distance of around 21 m and a braking distance of around 75 m.
- The relationship between speed and stopping distance can be inferred from graphed data.

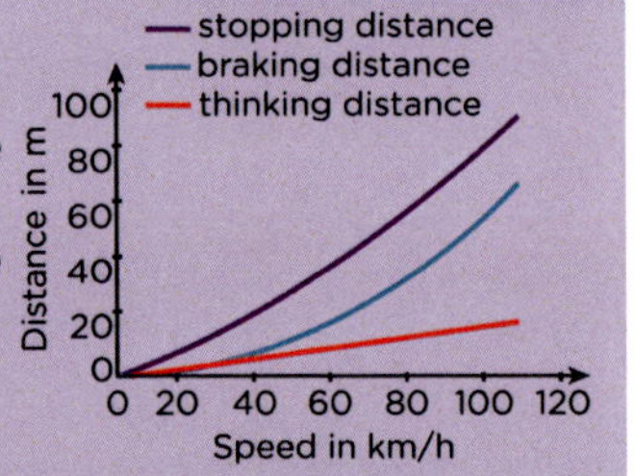

Braking force

All specs except: CIE, CCEA

- When a vehicle applies its brakes, the brakes apply a frictional (braking) force to the wheels. This frictional force does work to transfer kinetic energy away from the wheels and hence the vehicle. This energy is stored in the brakes and causes them to heat up.
- At higher speeds, the braking force will need to be larger, which will increase the work done by the braking force. This creates a risk of the brakes overheating and the driver losing control of the vehicle.
- For example, a 1500 kg car travelling on a motorway would need a braking force of ~6000 N to come to a stop, while a 35,000 kg truck travelling at the same speed would need a force of ~90,000 N to stop.

Momentum

Higher tier *All specs except: CCEA*

- Momentum is a vector quantity with a direction that is the same as that of the object's velocity.
- The momentum of an object is calculated as $\text{momentum} = \text{mass} \times \text{velocity}$. This can also be written as $p = mv$ where:
  - p is the object's momentum in kg m/s
  - m is its mass in kg
  - v is its velocity in m/s
- The principle of c**onservation of momentum** states that in a closed system, the total momentum before an event must be the same as the total momentum after an event. Examples of conservation of momentum include:
  - When a stationary gun fires a bullet, the gun recoils because it gains momentum equal and opposite to that of the bullet.

  - If a car travelling at speed crashes into a stationary car and they stick together, they will continue moving at reduced speed. If they originally had equal and opposite momenta, they will be brought to a stop.
  - If a snooker ball strikes a second ball and stops, the second snooker ball will start travelling with the first ball's initial momentum.

Calculating change in momentum

Higher tier *All specs except: CCEA*

- Calculations involving conservation of momentum can be solved by calculating the total momentum before and after an event and equating them.
  - If two objects are travelling in the same direction, their momentums are added.
  - If two objects are travelling in opposite directions, then their momentums are subtracted.

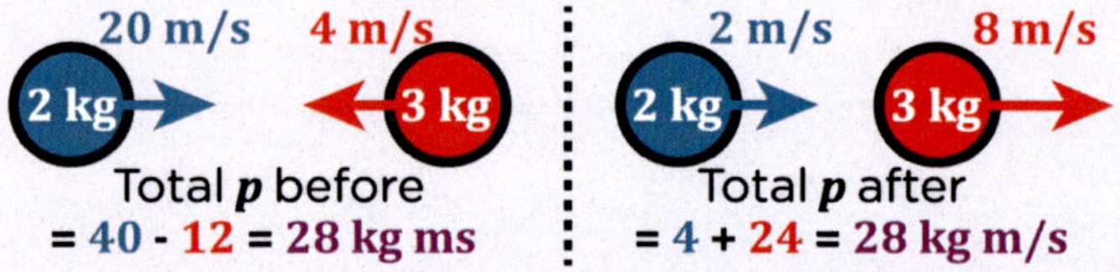

- Combining the equations $F = ma$ and $a = \frac{\Delta v}{t}$ leads to the relation between force and momentum: $F = \frac{m\Delta v}{t}$. This equation shows that force is equal to the rate of change of momentum.
- To stop moving, a force must be applied to change momentum to zero. Increasing the time it takes to stop will reduce the rate of change of momentum and the force. This principle is applied in numerous safety features such as crash mats and other cushioned surfaces, helmets, shin pads and other protective gear, seat belts and airbags in cars, and crumple zones, which collapse during a collision.

Properties of waves

Wave properties

- The **amplitude**, A, of a wave is the height of a wave, measured from its peak or trough to its undisturbed position.
- The **wavelength**, λ, of a wave is the distance between two equivalent points on it. It can be measured as the distance between two consecutive peaks or troughs.
- The **frequency**, f, of a wave is the number of waves produced per second or the number of waves that pass a point in a second measured in Hertz, Hz.
- The **period**, T, is the time it takes to produce one wave.
- Frequency and period are related by the equation period = 1 ÷ frequency or $T = \frac{1}{f}$.

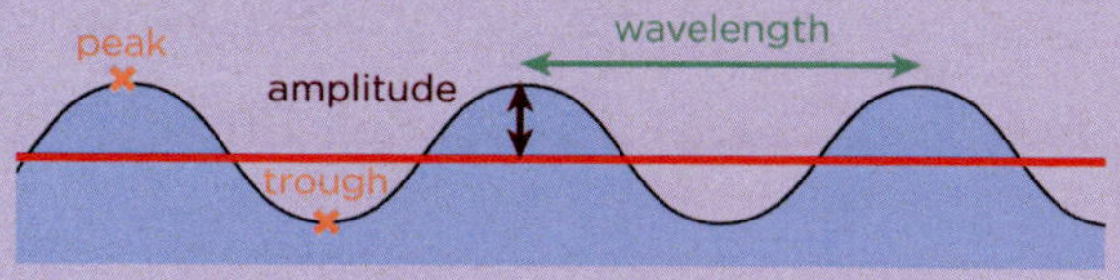

Transverse and longitudinal waves

- Waves are used to transport energy or information. When a wave travels through a medium such as water or air, it is the wave and not the medium that is travelling.
- **Transverse** waves are caused by vibrations that are perpendicular to their energy transfer. Examples of transverse waves are light and water ripples.
- **Longitudinal** waves are caused by vibrations that are parallel to the direction of energy transfer.
  - Longitudinal waves consist of compressions, where matter is pushed together, and rarefactions, where it is pulled apart.
  - Sound is an example of a longitudinal wave. It is produced by a vibrating object and travels through air by creating **compressions** and **rarefactions** in it.

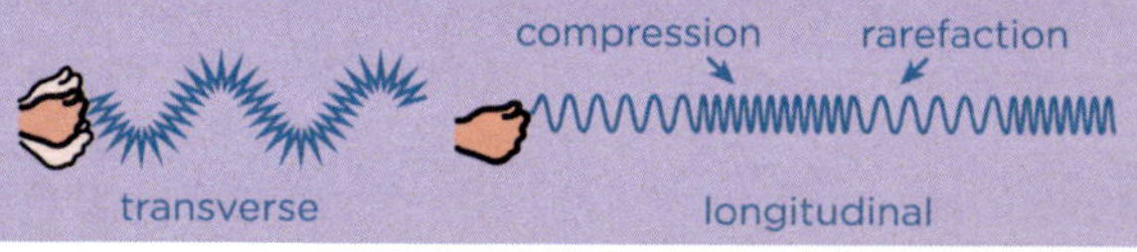

Wave speed

- Wave speed is the speed at which energy will be transferred by a wave, or the speed at which a wave moves, through a medium.
- Wave speed is given by wave speed = frequency × wavelength or $v = f\lambda$ where:
  - v is the wave speed in m/s
  - f is the frequency in Hz
  - λ is the wavelength in m
- Applications of wave speeds include measuring the wavelength and frequency of water ripples, reading the wavelength and frequency of sound waves from an oscilloscope, or recording the time it takes a sound echo to return to you after reflecting off a nearby building a known distance away.

Transmission

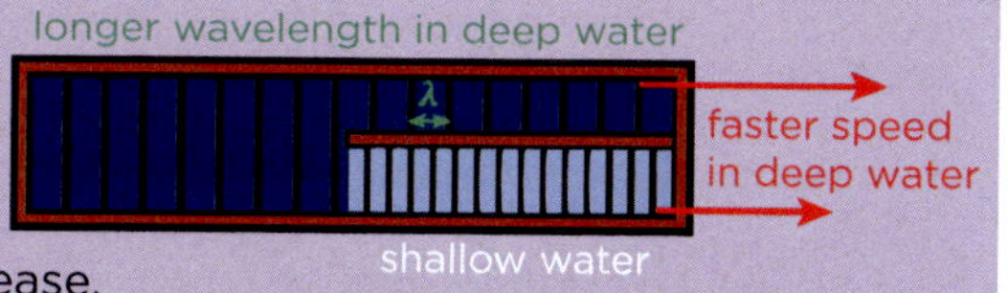

- Waves can travel from one medium to another. However, when they do so:
  - Their frequency will not change.
  - Their wavelength will increase or decrease.
  - So, the wave speed will increase or decrease.
- The wavelength and speed of water ripples will decrease when they enter shallower water.

Reflection and absorption

- When a wave reaches a boundary between two media, it can be transmitted, absorbed, or reflected.
- Typically, a wave that is reflected will also partially be transmitted.
- Waves will be reflected such that angle of incidence = angle of reflection.
  - This equation can be written as $i = r$, where i is the angle of incidence and r is the angle of reflection.
  - These angles are measured between the path of the wave and the normal to the boundary. The normal is a line drawn at 90° to its surface.

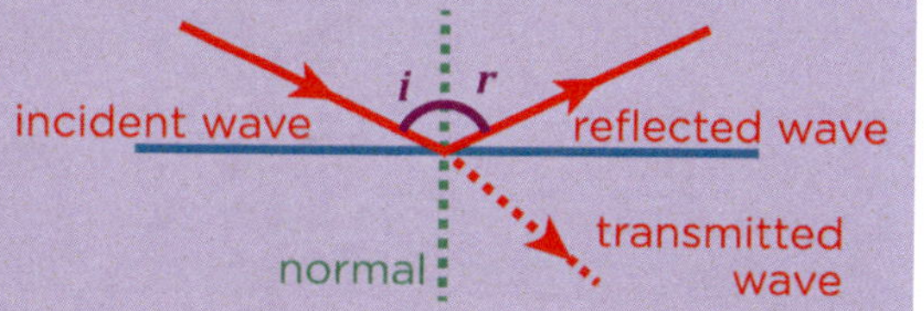

- We see an image in a mirror because reflected rays of light from an object appear to converge at a point inside the mirror.
- White and brightly coloured materials reflect a lot of light, while black and darkly coloured materials absorb a lot of light.

Sound waves

Higher tier

- Sound waves can travel through solids and liquids by causing vibrations in them.
- We detect sound waves using our ears:
  - When sound waves enter the ear, they cause the eardrum to vibrate.
  - This causes small bones in the ear to vibrate.
  - These connect to nerves, which send a signal to the brain, which interprets the vibrations as sound.
  - This process will only work for sound waves with frequencies between 20 Hz and 20,000 Hz.

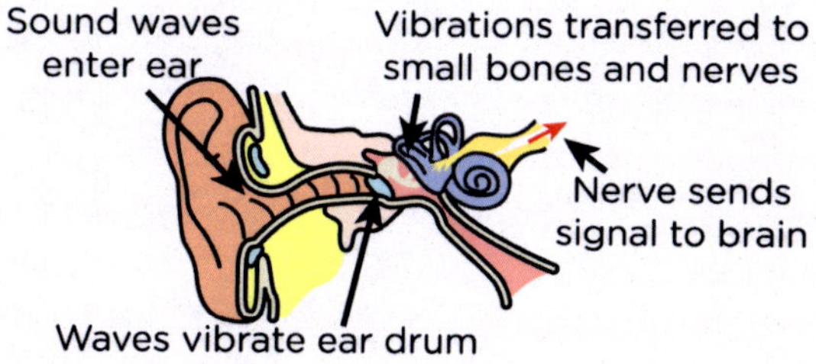

Electromagnetic waves

- Electromagnetic waves are transverse waves that transfer energy from a source to an absorber.
- The different types of electromagnetic waves form a continuous spectrum.
  - All electromagnetic waves will have the same speed in air or a vacuum.
  - This means that electromagnetic waves with larger wavelengths must have smaller frequencies.

Types of electromagnetic wave	
Wave	**Approximate wavelength range**
Gamma ray	10^{-12} m to 10^{-10} m
X-ray	10^{-10} m to 10^{-8} m
Ultraviolet	10^{-9} m to 10^{-7} m
Visible light	10^{-7} m
Infrared	10^{-6} m to 10^{-4} m
Microwave	10^{-4} m to 10^{-2} m
Radio wave	10^{-2} m to 10^{3} m

Applications of EM waves

Wave	Key property	Use
Radio	Can travel long distances and reflect off the ionosphere.	TV and radio signals
Microwaves	Can easily travel through the Earth's atmosphere.	Satellite communication
Microwaves	Absorbed by water to cause heating.	Cooking
Infrared	Emitted by warm bodies.	Heaters, cooking and infrared cameras
Visible light	Travels at high speed in glass.	Optical fibres
Ultraviolet	Absorbed by some materials and re-emitted as visible light.	Energy efficient lamps
Ultraviolet	Reacts with pigments in skin.	Tanning
Gamma	Penetrates skin/tissue, emitted by tracers.	Medical imaging
X-ray	Penetrates skin/tissue but absorbed by bone.	
Gamma/ X-ray	Damages and kills cancer cells.	Medical treatments

Radio waves

Higher tier

- Radio waves can be sent and received using aerials. An alternating current of high frequency in the transmitter causes electrons to oscillate up and down the aerial.
- This causes an electromagnetic wave, consisting of electric and magnetic fields oscillating at right angles to each other and the direction of energy transfer.
- When the wave reaches the receiving aerial, the fields cause electrons to oscillate up and down in it. This produces an alternating current of the same frequency as that in the transmitter.
- Radio waves can be used to send and receive signals for TV and radio broadcasts.

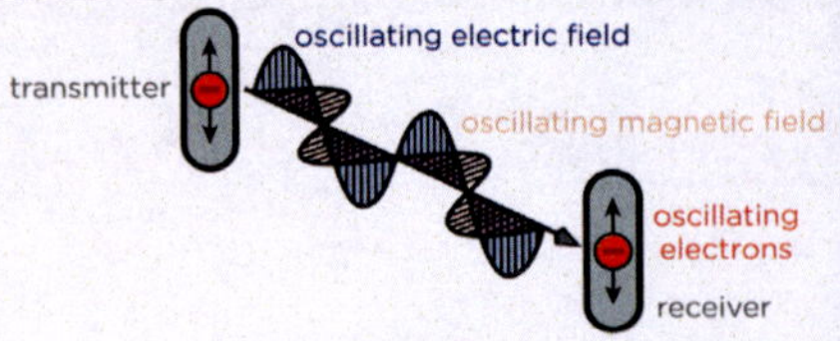

Ultrasound

Higher tier

- An ultrasound wave is a sound wave at a frequency above the range of human hearing. It is directed as a beam and the waves are partially reflected when they meet a boundary between two different media, and travel back to a detector.
- A computer records the reflected waves' intensities and the times it took for them to return. This information is used to produce an image or determine the depth.
- Ultrasound can be used for detection, such as with medical scans or sonar. It is especially useful for foetal scanning as it doesn't harm the patient or unborn baby.

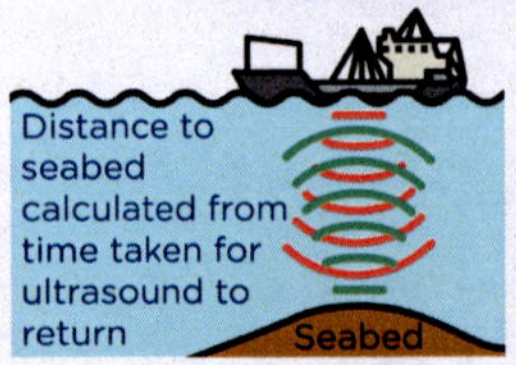

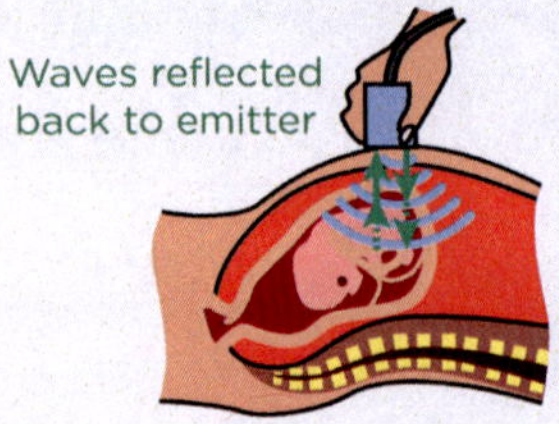

Seismic waves

Higher tier

- Earthquakes will produce seismic waves.
  - **P-waves** are **longitudinal** seismic waves. They will travel through solids and liquids at different speeds.
  - **S-waves** are **transverse** seismic waves. They can only travel through solids.
- The analysis of seismic waves and their reflections and transmissions inside the Earth has provided evidence to scientists about the Earth's structure and the properties of its three layers:
  - **Mantle:** solid outer layer of the Earth. All seismic waves can travel through it.
  - **Outer core:** liquid layer, meaning S-waves cannot travel through it.
  - **Inner core:** solid layer, meaning the P-waves that reach it will change speed.

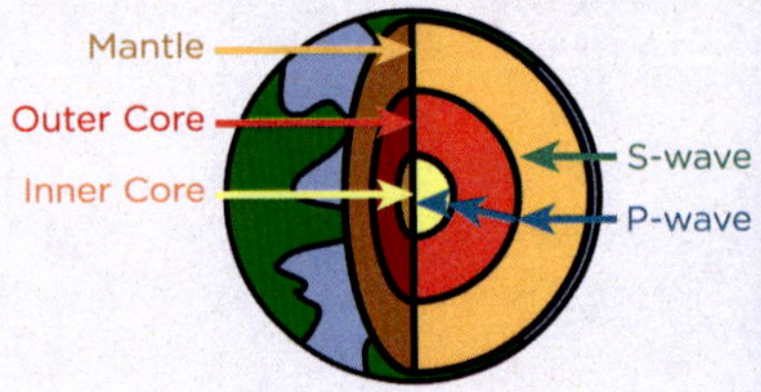

Refraction

- When an electromagnetic wave meets a surface, it can be:
  - Transmitted, causing the wave to pass through.
  - Absorbed, causing the wave to be stopped at the boundary.
  - Reflected, causing the wave to be redirected away from the boundary.
- The behaviour of the wave depends on its wavelength and the surface it is meeting.
  - Surfaces appear certain colours because those are the wavelengths of visible light that are reflected off them. All other colours are absorbed.
  - Metals reflect most waves but short wavelength waves, such as gamma waves, will pass through.
- Electromagnetic waves will change direction when transmitting into a different medium at an angle. This is called refraction.
  - Refraction can be shown on a ray diagram. A ray is a thin beam of electromagnetic waves, such as visible light.
  - The angle at which the ray enters a boundary is the angle of incidence. The angle at which it leaves is the angle of refraction. Both angles are measured against the normal, a line at 90° to the surface.

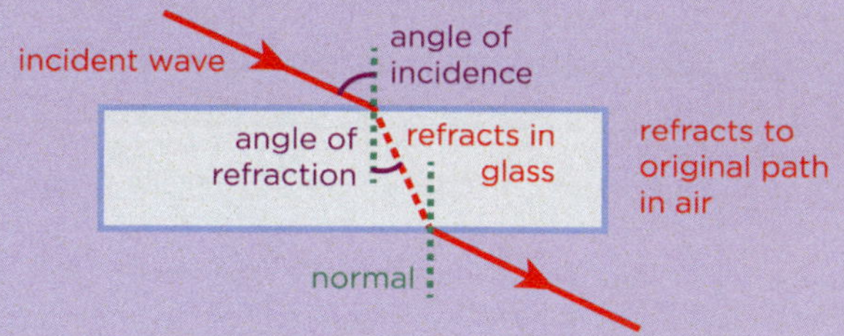

Refraction and speed

- The speed of an electromagnetic wave changes depending on the medium it is travelling through.
- Refraction is caused by light changing speed as it enters a different medium.
  - If light slows down it will bend towards the normal.
  - If light speeds up it will bend away from the normal.
- Refraction can also be observed in water waves when entering a shallower part of water. The waves will slow down with shorter wavelengths, and change direction.

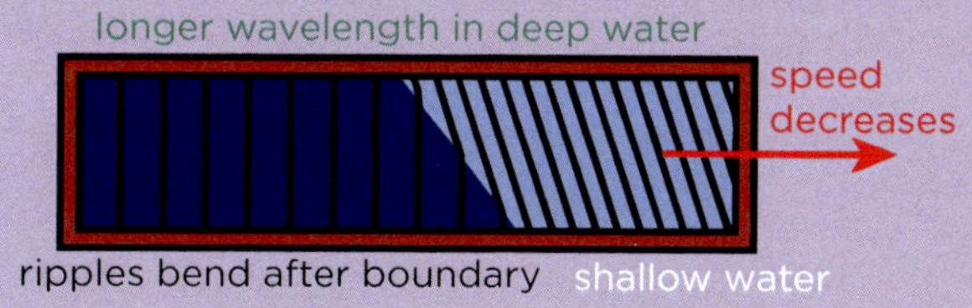

Lenses

All specs except: WJEC

- Lenses use refraction to redirect light and form an image.
  - Convex lenses will cause light rays from a distant object to converge at a point to form a real image. This image can be seen by placing a sheet of paper on the other side of the lens.
  - Concave lenses will diverge light away from a point to form a virtual image. This image will make us think an object is somewhere it is not and cannot be formed on paper.
  - Convex lenses can also form virtual images of objects close to them.
- Light rays passing through the lens parallel to its principal axis will converge to a single point. This is the principal focus of the lens.
  - The focal length is the distance between the principal focus and the lens.
  - As a concave lens causes rays to diverge, the focus is instead a virtual focus that is on the same side of the lens as the original rays.

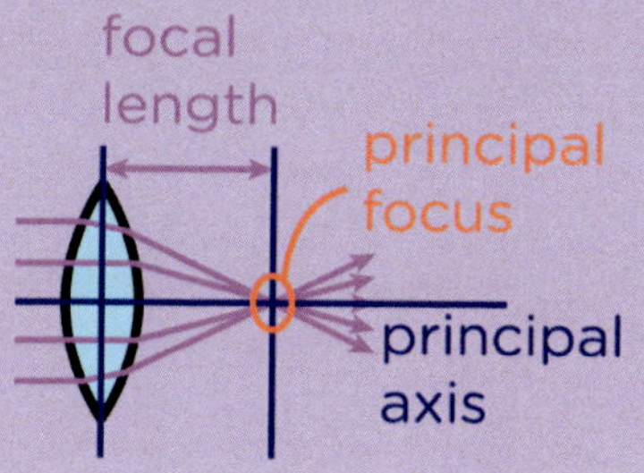

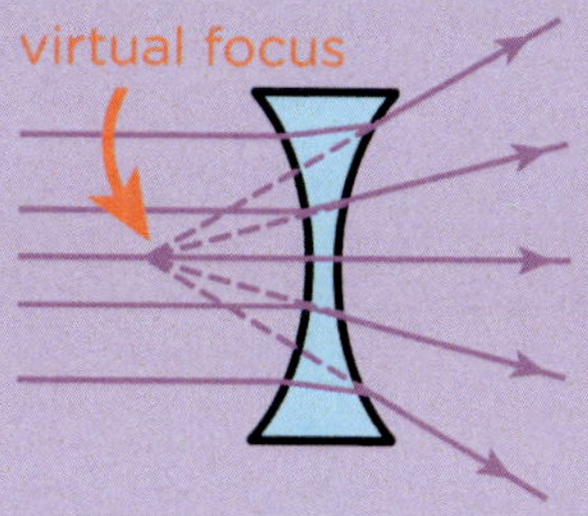

Magnification

All specs except: WJEC

- The magnification of a lens is a ratio of the size of the image it produces compared to the size of the object.
  - Magnification is a unitless quantity.
  - A magnification greater than 1 means the image will be larger than the object. A magnification of less than 1 means it will be smaller.
- Magnification can be calculated from a ray diagram using the formula $\text{magnification} = \text{image height} \div \text{object height}$.
- Convex lenses can produce magnified images when the object is placed between the lens and its focal point.
- Magnified images can be real and inverted (e.g. when object is beyond the focal point) or virtual and upright (e.g. within the focal length).

Light, colour, and ray diagrams

SNAPREVISE

Visible light

- Humans are only capable of seeing visible light.
- Visible light consists of a spectrum of different colours. Each colour corresponds to a small range of wavelengths. Red light has the longest wavelength and the lowest frequency. Violet light has the shortest wavelength and the highest frequency.

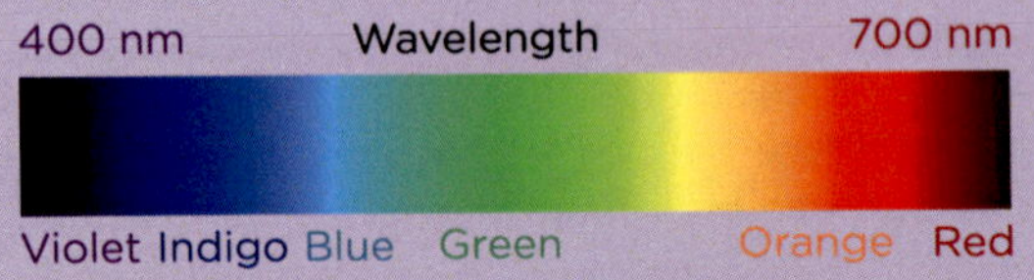

- Specular reflection is when light reflects off a smooth surface. Diffuse reflection is when light reflects at different angles off a rough surface
  - Light reflects in a single direction in specular reflection to form a clear image, such as with a mirror.
  - Light will scatter after diffuse reflection. We cannot see an image but can see the colour of the surface it reflected from.

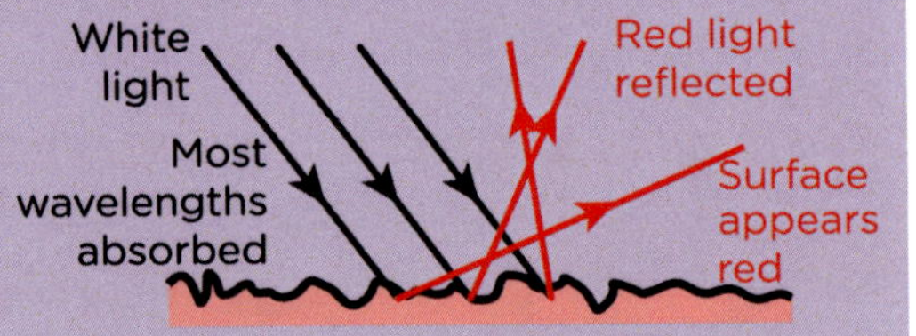

- Transparent materials will allow visible light to pass through. Translucent materials will also allow light to pass through but objects can't be as clearly seen through them (e.g. frosted glass).

Seeing colour

- Light can be split into a spectrum by using a glass prism. This is because each wavelength of light refracts differently in the prism.

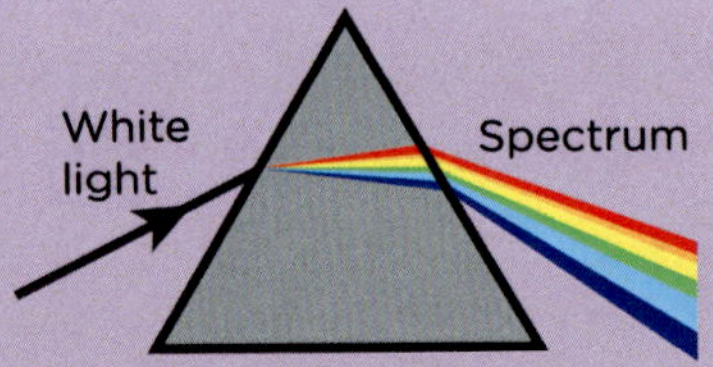

- Opaque materials are ones that won't allow visible light to pass through.
  - Certain wavelengths of light will be reflected while the rest will be absorbed. The material will appear to be a colour corresponding to the reflected wavelengths.
  - White materials will reflect all wavelengths of visible light while black materials will absorb all wavelengths.
- Colour filters are transparent materials that only allow certain wavelengths of visible light to pass through. The other wavelengths are absorbed. They are used to isolate certain colours in light.

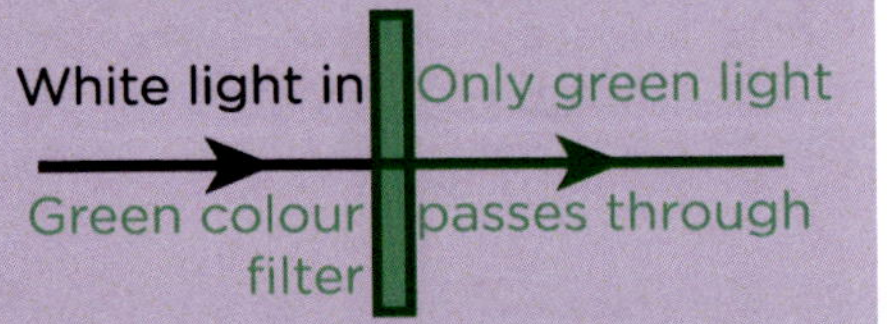

Ray diagrams

Higher tier

All specs except: WJEC

- Ray diagrams are used to determine the position, size, orientation, and nature (real or virtual) of an image formed by a lens by tracing the paths of light rays from an object.
- Objects are typically assumed to be placed on the principal axis, with the object extending vertically above the axis to simplify the construction of the diagram.
- The top of the image is located at the point where the refracted rays from the top of the object intersect (or appear to diverge from) after passing through the lens.
- To construct a ray diagram for a convex lens, **three principal rays** are usually drawn from the top of the object:
  - A ray parallel to the principal axis travels to the lens and is refracted through the focal point on the opposite side.
  - A ray through the centre of the lens (optical centre) continues in a straight line without deviation.
  - A ray directed toward the focal point on the object's side of the lens is refracted by the lens to emerge parallel to the principal axis.
- The **nature of the image** depends on the object's distance from the lens:
  - If the image forms on the opposite side of the lens from the object, it is a real image (can be projected on a screen).
  - If the rays diverge and the image appears to form on the same side as the object, it is a virtual image (cannot be projected).
- The **orientation** of the image depends on where the rays converge:
  - If they meet below the principal axis, the image is inverted.
  - If they meet above the axis (as in virtual images), the image is upright.
- The size of the image compared to the object can be magnified, diminished, or same size, depending on the object's distance from the lens relative to the focal length.

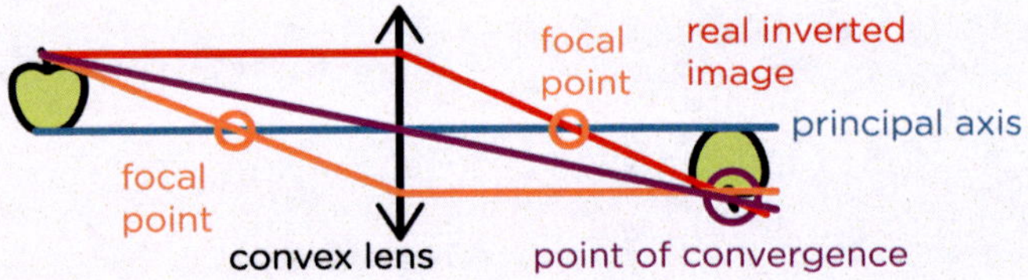

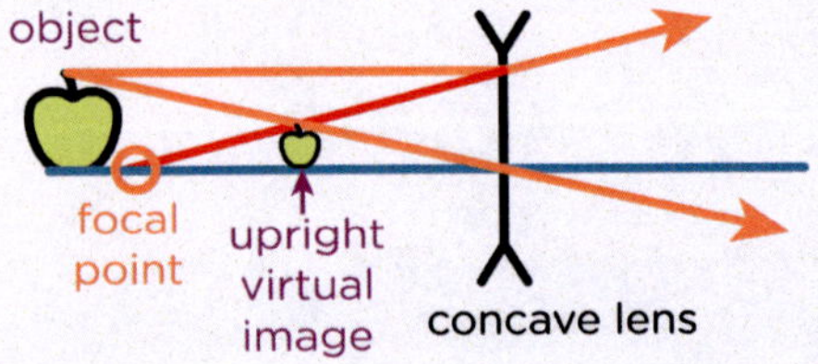

Absorbing and emitting infrared radiation

SNAPREVISE

Hazardous waves

- Electromagnetic waves can be produced when changes occur within atoms or their nuclei, such as during **radioactive decay** or when **electrons move between energy levels.**
- **Gamma rays** are emitted from the nucleus of an atom when it loses excess nuclear energy, often after alpha or beta decay, and are the most penetrating and energetic type of electromagnetic radiation.
- Atoms can also absorb electromagnetic radiation, which can cause electrons to move to higher energy levels. These changes can later result in re-emission of electromagnetic waves.
- Certain types of electromagnetic radiation, specifically ultraviolet (UV), X-rays, and gamma rays, are particularly hazardous to living tissue because they carry enough energy to ionise atoms, potentially damaging or mutating DNA within cells.
  - **Ultraviolet (UV) radiation** can lead to premature ageing of the skin, sunburn, and an increased risk of skin cancer.
    - UV exposure is primarily from the sun and artificial sources like tanning beds.
    - Protection includes wearing sunblock, covering skin, and avoiding prolonged sun exposure.
  - **X-rays and gamma rays** are widely used in medical diagnostics and treatment.
    - For example, X-rays are used for imaging bones and gamma rays are used in cancer radiotherapy.
    - Excessive or repeated exposure can be harmful for both patients and technicians.
    - Medical professionals minimise exposure by using lead shields, limiting frequency of procedures, and ensuring only essential scans are performed.
- The risk from exposure to hazardous waves is quantified using radiation dose, measured in sieverts (Sv). This takes into account:
  - The type of radiation (e.g. gamma rays are more penetrating than UV)
  - The amount (intensity) of radiation
  - The duration of exposure
- Monitoring and controlling exposure to hazardous radiation is critical in fields such as healthcare, nuclear power, and aviation, to protect both workers and the public.

Temperature change and radiation

Higher tier

- If an object is at a constant temperature, then it is absorbing and emitting radiation at the same rate:
  - If it absorbs radiation faster than it can emit, then its temperature is rising, such as with an ice cube in a warm room.
  - If it emits radiation faster than it can absorb, then its temperature is decreasing, such as with a lump of hot coal in a cool room.
- The temperature of the Earth depends on how it absorbs radiation from the sun and re-emits it into space.
  - One side of Earth is facing the Sun, so it absorbs a lot of radiation. The other side faces away from the Sun, so it doesn't absorb any radiation but is still emitting it. So, the Earth's surface warms up during the day and cools at night.
  - Less radiation is incident to the Earth at its poles than on the equator. This is why the equator is very hot and the poles are very cold.

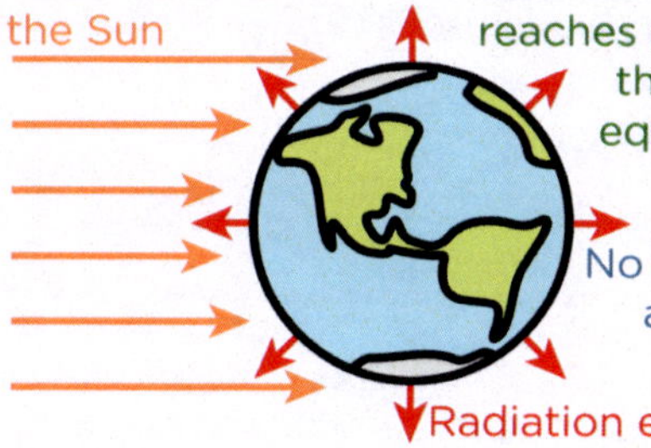

Absorption and emission of infrared radiation

All specs except: WJEC

- All bodies will absorb and emit infrared radiation. This is true for objects of any temperature, but hotter objects will emit more radiation per second.
- At high temperatures, the object will also emit red visible light. As the temperature increases, it also emits light of shorter wavelengths, eventually emitting white light.

Black body radiation

Only: AQA, Eduqas

- A perfect black body is an object that will not reflect or transmit any radiation directed onto it, only absorb it. Black bodies are also perfect emitters of radiation as good absorbers are good emitters.
- Perfect black bodies only exist in theory, but there are objects that absorb almost all radiation directed at them.

Magnetic fields

Magnetic poles

- Certain materials, such as iron, can experience magnetic forces.
- These are **non-contact forces.**
- Magnetic forces are strongest near **magnetic poles.**
  - Poles are labelled north or south depending on the direction they would eventually face if the magnet could freely turn.
  - Every magnet must have one of each pole. Both poles are as strong as each other.
  - Like poles will experience a repulsive force when brought near each other while unlike poles will attract.
- Permanent magnets are those that produce magnetic fields. Induced magnets are materials that become magnets when in another magnetic field.
  - The poles of the induced magnet will always be so that it feels an attractive force in the field. Repulsive forces can only be experienced by two permanent magnets.
  - When an induced magnet leaves the magnetic field, it will lose its magnetism very quickly.

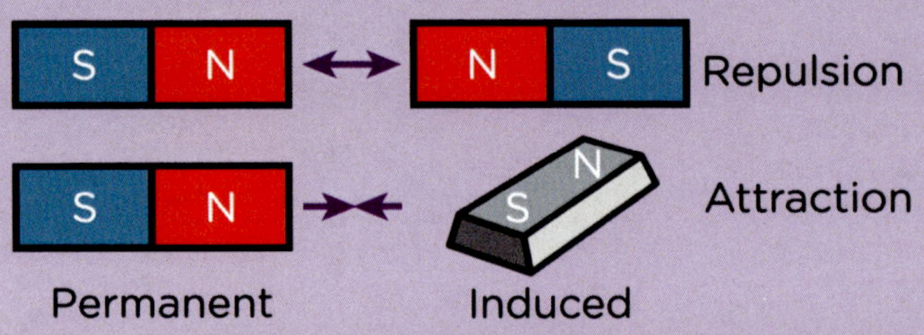

Magnetic fields

- A magnetic field is the region around a magnet where other magnets or magnetic materials will experience a force.
- Magnetic fields can be visualised using field lines:
  - The lines all point from a north pole to a south pole. This represents the direction of the force a north pole would experience in the field.
  - The strength of the field is indicated by how close together field lines are. They will be closest near to the poles of the magnet.
  - Field lines should not cross or touch each other.

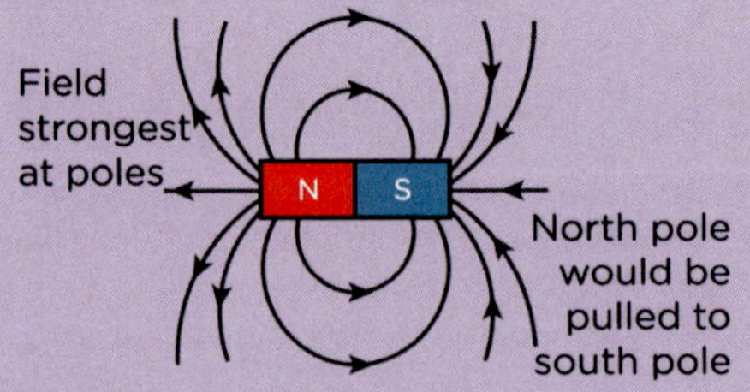

Compasses

- There is a permanent magnetic field around the Earth. Its poles align with the geographical North and South poles.
- A compass contains a small permanent magnet that can freely rotate so that it aligns with the Earth's magnetic field.
- The North pole of the compass will point north due to an attractive force. This means the north pole of the Earth's magnetic field is actually at the South Pole.

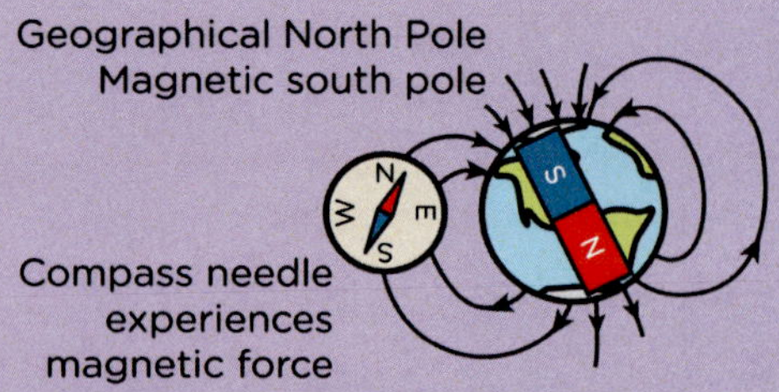

Field around a wire

- A magnetic field is produced when a current flows through a conducting wire. This field takes a circular shape.
- The field is strongest close to the wire. Increasing the current also increases the strength of the field.
- The direction of the field can be determined using the **right-hand grip rule.**
  - Hold out your right hand and point your thumb so that it points in the direction of the current.
  - Curl your fingers. The direction they point in is the direction of the magnetic field.

Solenoids

- A solenoid consists of a wire coiled into numerous loops.
  - The magnetic fields from each loop on the coil combine to form a field similar in shape to a bar magnet outside the coils and uniform inside them.
  - The strength of this field can be increased by increasing the current or using more loops on the coil.
- An electromagnet is a solenoid with an iron core within the coil.
  - The iron core further increases the strength of the magnetic field.
  - Electromagnets are useful as their strong magnetic field can be switched on or off very quickly.

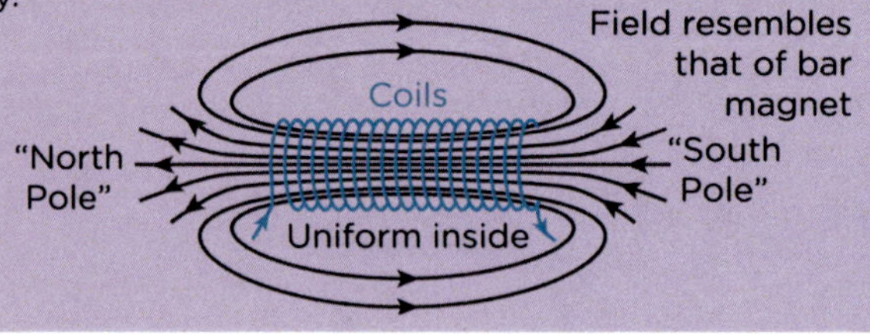

Motor effect, generator effect, and transformers

The motor effect

Higher tier

- The motor effect is when a conductor carrying a current through a magnetic field experiences a force from the magnet and conductor fields squashing against each other.

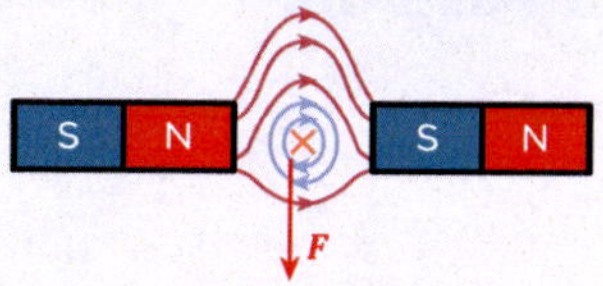

- The direction of the force on a wire can be determined using **Fleming's Left-Hand Rule.** This is done by holding your thumb, first finger and second finger out at right angles to each other with your first finger should point in the direction of the field, and your second finger should point in the direction of the current in the wire. Your thumb will then point in the direction of the force.

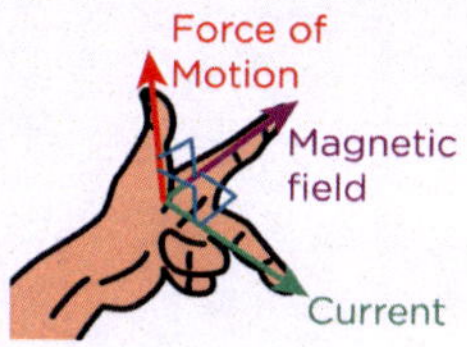

- The magnitude of the force on a wire at right angles to the field is given by force = magnetic flux density × current × length .
  - **Magnetic flux density** is a measure of a magnetic field's strength or how close together its field lines are. It is measured in Tesla, T.
  - This equation can also be written as $F = BIL$ where F is the force the wire experiences in N, B is the magnetic flux density of the field in T, I is the current in the wire in A, and L is the length of the wire within the field in m.

Electric motors

Higher tier

- An electric motor utilises the motor effect to convert electrical energy to kinetic energy through rotation:
  - A rectangular coil of wire is placed in a magnetic field so that it can freely rotate around a pivot.
  - When a current flows through the coil, the two sides of the coil experience vertical forces in opposite directions. This causes the coil to rotate.

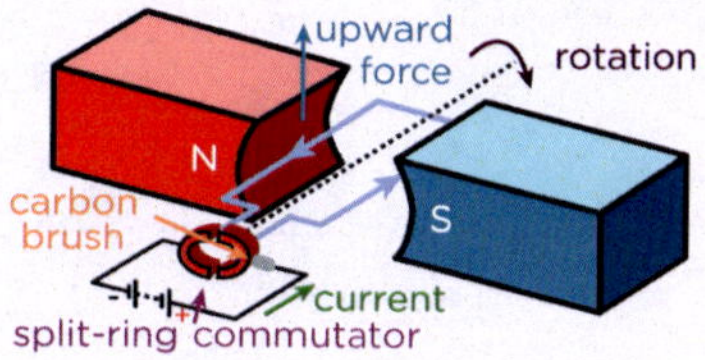

- The coil receives current from a circuit connected to it with a split-ring commutator.
- This rotates while always maintaining a connection through the use of two carbon brushes. The split ring switches brush periodically so the current reverses and the forces on the coil are always in the same direction.

Loudspeakers

All specs except: WJEC, CCEA **Higher tier**

- A loudspeaker or pair of headphones generates sound waves using the motor effect where an alternating current flows through a coil in a magnetic field, causing the coil and magnet to experience a force.
- The coil pulls on a cone, which generates vibrations in the air as a sound wave.
- Variations in the frequency and size of the current change the motion of the cone, creating different sound waves.

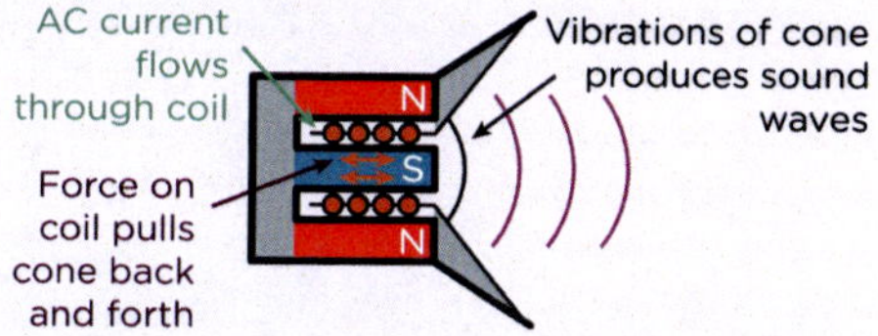

The generator effect

Higher tier

- A **potential difference** is induced in a conductor when it moves relative to a magnetic field or there is a change in the field. A current is induced if the conductor is connected to a complete circuit. This field opposes the change causing the **generator effect** and is the main method of **generating electricity**.
- Reversing the motion of the conductor or the polarity of the field reverses the direction of the potential difference.
- The size of an induced potential difference can be increased by increasing the speed of motion of the conductor or rate of change of the field, using a stronger magnetic field, or using a longer length of conductor or coiling it.
- An **alternator** uses the generator effect to produce an alternating current when a coil turns in a magnetic field, inducing a potential difference in it. The coil connects to a circuit using a pair of slip rings, inducing a current.
- The strength and direction of the current vary with time. It will be strongest when the coil is perpendicular to the field. Increasing speed of rotation increases peak potential difference and frequency.

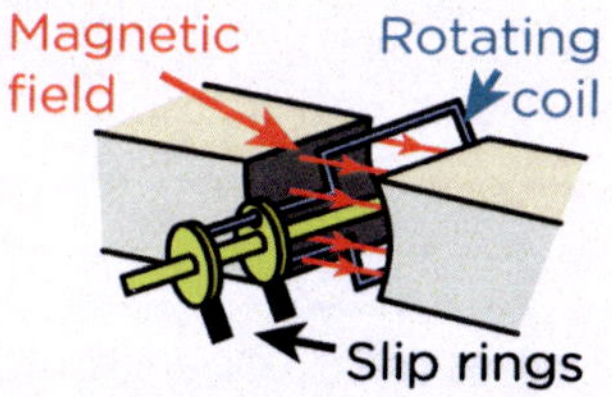

- A **dynamo** functions similarly to an alternator but uses a slip ring communicator instead of a pair of slip rings. So, it will instead produce a varying direct current.
- **Microphones** contain a coil that vibrates around a magnet when sound waves are directed at it. This generates a current that converts the sound waves to an electrical signal. This signal can be sent to a loudspeaker to project the sound.

Transformers

Higher tier

- A transformer consists of two coils wrapped around an iron core. When an alternating current flows through one coil, it induces a magnetic field around it.
  - This magnetic field is periodically changing direction and is concentrated by the iron core, so it induces an alternating current in the other coil.
  - An iron core is used as it is easily magnetised.
- Transformers are used to change an alternating potential difference.
  - **Step-up transformers** increase potential difference by having more turns on their secondary coils.
  - **Step-down transformers** decrease potential difference by having more turns on their primary coils.

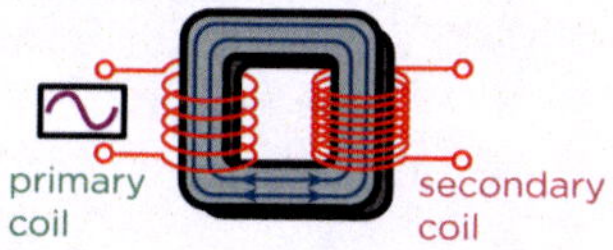

- The transformer equation states that the ratio of potential differences and turns in the coils of a transformer are equal: $\frac{V_p}{V_s} = \frac{n_p}{n_s}$ where V_p and V_s are the potential differences in the primary and secondary coils respectively in V, and n_p and n_s are the number of turns in the primary and secondary coils respectively.
- If a transformer is 100% efficient, then there are no energy losses and the input power to the primary coil is equal to the output power from the secondary coil. This can be written as $V_s \times I_s = V_p \times I_p$.

Space

SNAPREVISE

The Solar System

- The solar system consists of:
  - A star, orbited by planets, called the Sun, which releases energy to its surroundings.
  - Four planets close to the Sun made from rock: Mercury, Venus, Earth and Mars.
  - Five planets further from the Sun made of gas: Jupiter, Saturn, Uranus and Neptune.
  - Dwarf planets further from the Sun, including Pluto.
  - Moons that orbit planets.
- The Sun is part of a group of over 200,000 million stars in the Milky Way galaxy.

Life of a star

- All stars start life in the same way a cloud of dust and gas, called a **nebula**, is pulled together by gravity. Collisions between molecules generate heat to form a ball of gas called a **protostar**.
- When enough matter is pulled together, the high temperature of the star allows hydrogen to collide through **fusion**. The energy released from these reactions balances the gravitational forces trying to collapse the star. This is a **main-sequence star**. When the star runs out of hydrogen to fuse, it starts to collapse under gravitational forces. This allows helium to fuse into heavier elements.
- For **low-mass stars** (similar size to the Sun): the fusion of helium causes the star to expand into a **red giant**. When the red giant runs out of helium to fuse, it collapses into a **white dwarf**. The white dwarf eventually cools into a **black dwarf**.
- For **high-mass stars**: helium can fuse into even heavier elements, causing the star to expand into a red supergiant. The heaviest element made in the process is iron.
- When the **red supergiant** runs out of fuel, it will collapse again. This causes the iron to fuse into even heavier elements, causing energy to be released in an explosion called a **supernova**. All elements heavier than iron were originally created and released in supernovae.
- Alternatively, the star can collapse into a highly condensed ball of matter called a **neutron star**, or it can collapse into a microscopic point, forming a **black hole**.

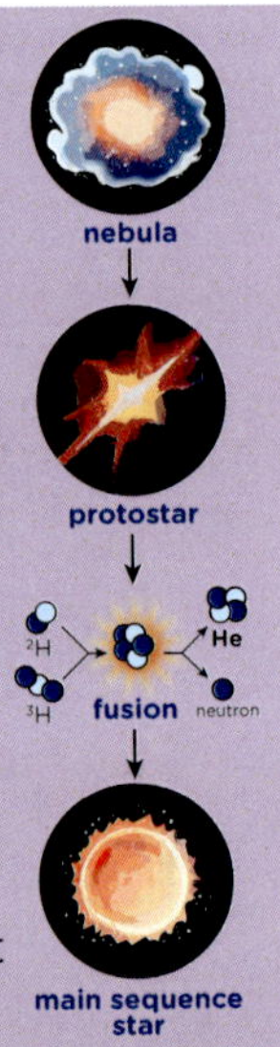

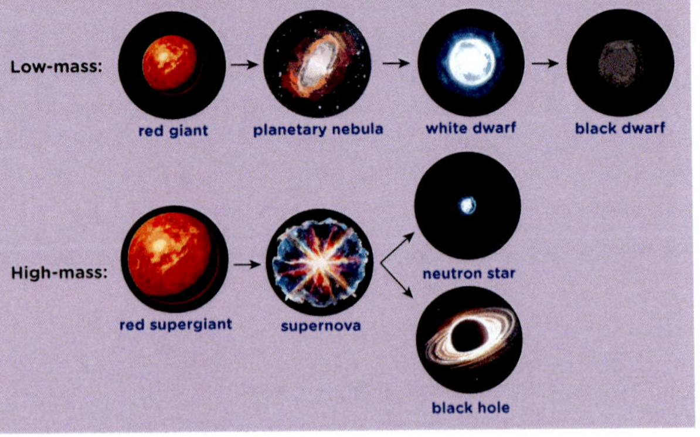

Orbits and satellites

- Planets and satellites are held in orbits by gravitational forces. Satellites experience forces with planets and planets experience forces with the Sun.
- Satellites can be natural, like a moon, or artificial, like the International Space Station.
- Gravitational forces keep planets and satellites travelling in circular paths.
- The speed of an orbiting object is $\text{speed} = (2\pi \times \text{orbital radius}) \div \text{period of orbit}$.
- If the speed of the orbiting object changes, then its orbital radius must also change. If it doesn't, then the orbit will become unstable.

Red-shift

- Sounds appear to have a higher or lower pitch depending on if the source is moving towards or away from us. This is because the sound waves are being compressed or stretched respectively, changing their wavelength and frequency.
- A similar phenomenon occurs with light from extremely fast-moving sources.
  - Analysing the light from distant galaxies shows that its wavelength is longer than expected. This is called red-shift.
  - This suggests the galaxy is moving away from the Earth.
  - Furthermore, the further the galaxy is away, the greater the red-shift. This suggests the further away a galaxy is, the faster it is moving.

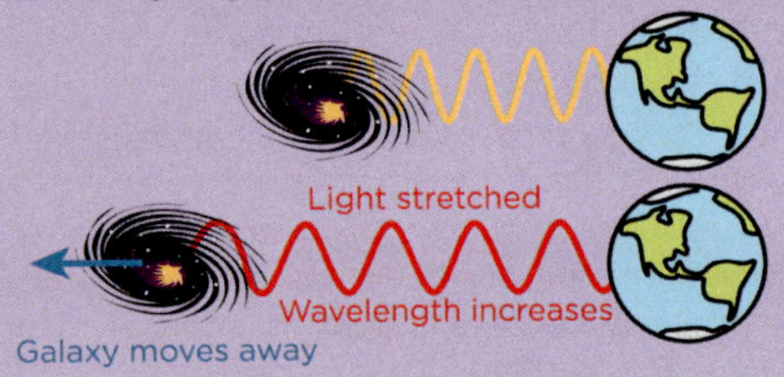

The Big Bang Theory

- Observations of red-shift support the Big Bang theory for the origin of the universe.
  - Matter and all space exploded from a very small, extremely hot and dense region around 13.8 billion years ago, creating the universe.
  - The extremely hot matter from this explosion eventually cooled and was pulled together by gravity, creating stars and galaxies.
  - The energy from the explosion is making the universe continue to expand, pushing galaxies apart from each other.
- It was expected that gravity would slow down the rate of the universe's expansion. However, recent observations of supernovae suggest that this rate is actually increasing. This has led to the theories of dark matter and dark energy, which influence this expansion.

SNAPREVISE

Scientific processes

- Scientific ideas are not accepted until there is evidence to back them up.
  - Theories, theorems and experimental results are published in scientific journals. These undergo peer review by the scientific community before they are accepted.
  - Scientists will also repeat experiments described in journals to confirm their results are valid.
  - Some scientific ideas considered correct today were not initially accepted until decades after they were first published, such as Darwin's theory of evolution.
- Currently accepted scientific theories and models are the ones that best fit the current evidence and knowledge of the universe. They may be disproven in future.
- Scientific ideas that are reported in popular media before verification and peer review can lead to negative opinions of science.

Apparatus and equipment

Apparatus	Symbol
Bunsen burner: provides a constant flow of heat to a substance	
Beaker: stores water or other fluids. Other containers like canonical flasks may also be used depending on the experiment.	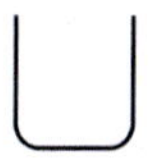
Test tube: holds a small amount of liquid. Larger tubes for heating are called boiling tubes.	
Tripod: a stand that a Bunsen burner can be placed under. Gauze can be used to place a beaker on top.	
Clamp stand: can be used in conjunction with clamps and bosses to suspend test tubes and other equipment in the air.	
Funnel: directs liquid into a test tube or another container.	

- Various equipment can be used to take measurements during experiments. More precise equipment will lead to better results.
- Choosing the correct equipment and calibrating regularly can help ensure reliable results and reduce random errors.

Equipment	Used to measure
Ruler	Length
Measuring cylinder	Volume
Stopwatch	Time
Thermometer	Temperature
Pan balance/scale	Mass

Variables

- Scientific experiments are performed to determine the relationship between two or more variables.
- An **independent variable** is a variable that is manually changed. An experiment should have only one independent variable.
- A **dependent variable** is a variable that will change as a result of a change in the independent variable.
- The dependent and independent variables are measured to determine the relationship between them.
- A **control variable** is a variable that must be kept the same throughout the experiment to make the test fair.
- Changing a control variable will make it unclear if that change or a change in the independent variable is responsible for a change in the dependent variable.

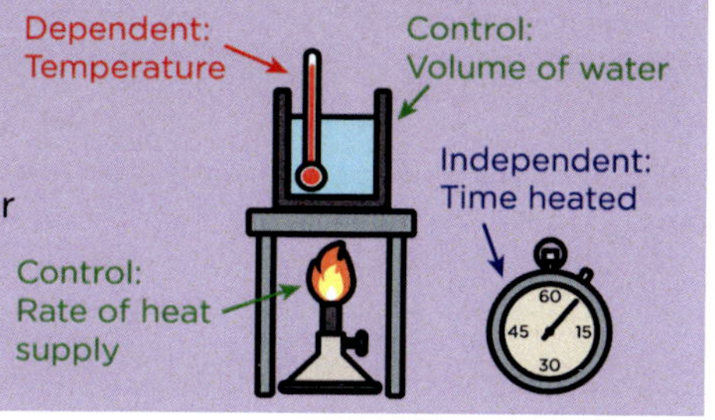

Safe experiments

- Measures should be taken so experiments are conducted safely.
- Sensible protective clothing should be worn, including **goggles** or safety visors to protect the eyes from harmful substances, **lab coats** to protect clothing from damage or harmful substances, and **gloves** when handling hazardous materials. Long hair should also be tied back so it is not a hazard.

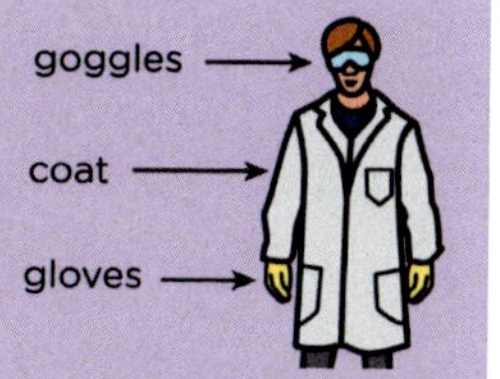

- Steps should be taken to ensure **Bunsen burners** are used safely: using a heatproof mat underneath, and using **tongs** for any substances/equipment that is heated. The burner should be left on a yellow flame and gas taps should be turned off when not in use.

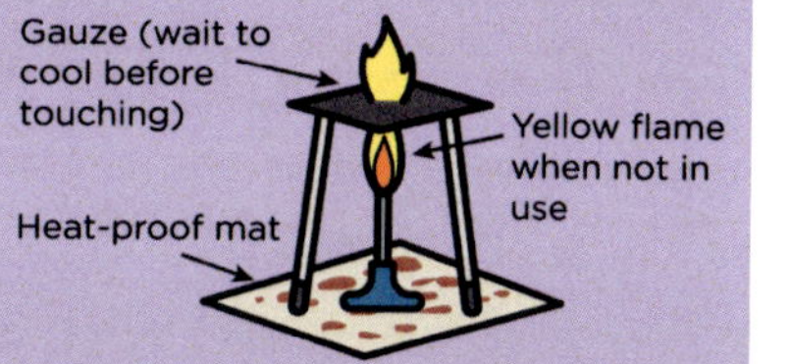

- Hazardous substances, such as chemicals or radioactive materials, should be handled with care and stored when not in use.
  - Containers should be correctly marked with their hazards (e.g. skin irritant).
  - Particularly dangerous substances should not be handled directly.
  - Flammable substances should be kept away from naked flames (e.g. ethanol).
- Biohazards, such as bacterial cultures, should be handled with care.
  - Aseptic techniques should be used when preparing bacterial cultures.
  - Disinfectant should be used after exposure to biohazards to prevent contamination.
  - Avoid contact with skin of stains (e.g. Toluidine blue or DCPIP).
  - Hands should be washed after handling biohazards or unsterilised samples .
- All equipment should be checked regularly.
  - Clamps and bosses should be tightly secured.
  - Electrical equipment should be inspected to ensure they have no live wires.

Science skills: Presenting and using data

SNAPREVISE

Presenting data

- **Frequency tables** are used to record results from experiments. The first column should be the independent variable, and headers should include units

Example frequency table					
Independent variable, x (s)	Measured variable, y (m)				Calculated dependent variable, y^2 (m^2)
	1	2	3	Mean	
1	1.2	1.4	1.3	1.3	1.7
2	2.8	2.6	3	2.8	7.8
3	3.7	3.2	3.8	3.6	12.7

- **Bar charts** are used to compare categoric variables to continuous variables.

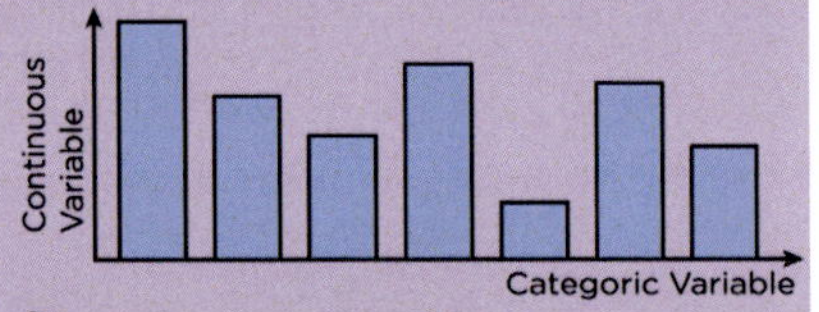

- **Histograms** show how a set of continuous data fits into grouped categories.
  - The height of each bar represents the frequency density.
  - The area of each bar is proportional to the number of data values in the group.
  - The bars should all be touching.

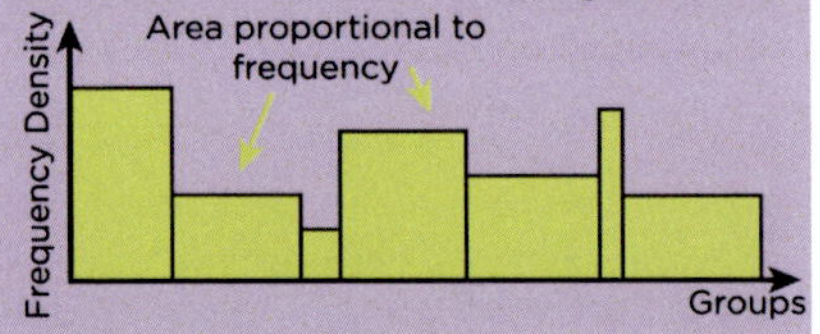

- **Line graphs** compare two continuous variables.
  - Recorded data is plotted onto a graph. The x and y coordinates of each point correspond to a value for the independent and dependent variable, respectively.
  - A smooth curve is drawn to show the general relationship. This should be close to as many points as possible, excluding outliers.

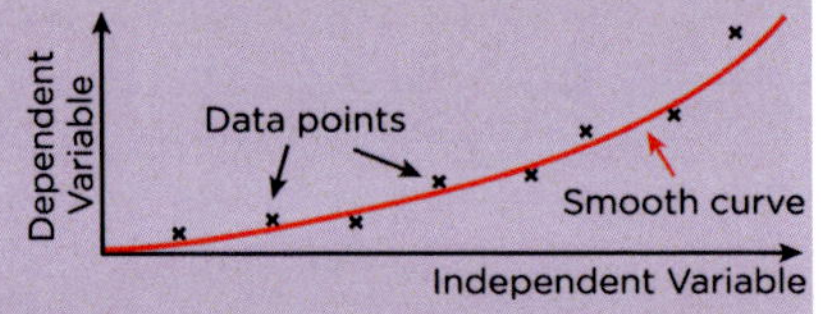

Rounding and standard form

- To round a value to a certain number of significant figures: identify the first non-zero digit in the value and count the number of digits after this. You will round this last digit up or down depending on if the next digit is greater than or equal to 5. Remove all digits outside the count (e.g. 0.005486 ≈ 0.0589 to 3 sig figs).
- Calculated values should be given to a number of significant figures equal to the lowest number of significant figures from the numbers used (e.g. the answer to 583 × 3.4 should be given to 2 sig figs.
- Values are rounded to the point where they should be the same as the true value rounded to that many significant figures.
- Standard form is used to write out very large or very small rounded numbers.
  - Write a number between 1 and 10 and multiply it by a power of 10. This can be positive or negative depending on if the number is big or small. Each multiplication by 10 moves the decimal point one digit to the left or right.
  - E.g. 158000 = 1.58×10^5 and 0.00158 = 1.58×10^{-3}.

Equations

- Equations show the relationship between scientific variables under certain conditions. To use an equation to find an unknown value using an equation:
  - Rearrange equation algebraically to make the unknown variable the subject.
  - Substitute in the values in the correct places, ensuring the units are the ones needed for the equation, and calculate the unknown value.
- Formula triangles can be used to help understand how to rearrange equations.
  - Cover the part of the triangle for the unknown value.
  - Divide the top value by the bottom value, or multiply the bottom values.

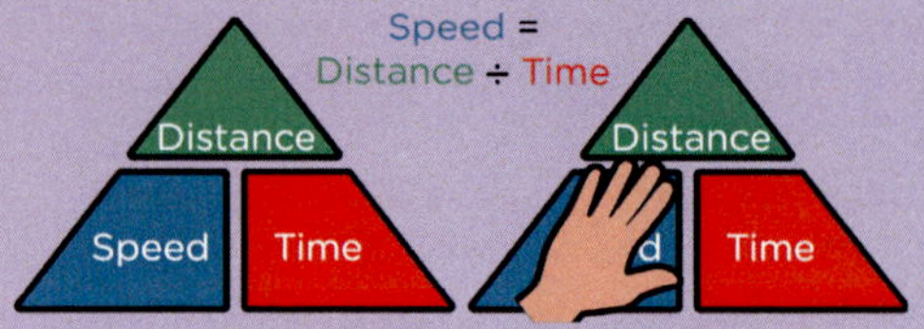

Interpreting graphs

- The **gradient** of a straight line of best fit can give information about the relationship between two variables in a graph.
- To calculate the gradient, choose two points on the lines as far apart as possible such that their x and y values are easy to read and calculate the differences in the two x and the two y values. The gradient will be **difference in y ÷ difference in x.**

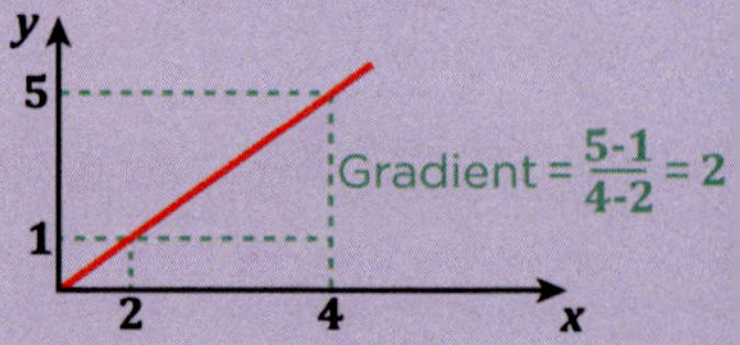

- A curved **line of best fit** has a changing gradient. The gradient at a particular point can be calculated by drawing a tangent.
  - A **tangent** is a straight line that only just brushes against the point on the curve.
  - The gradient of the curve is the gradient of this straight-line tangent.

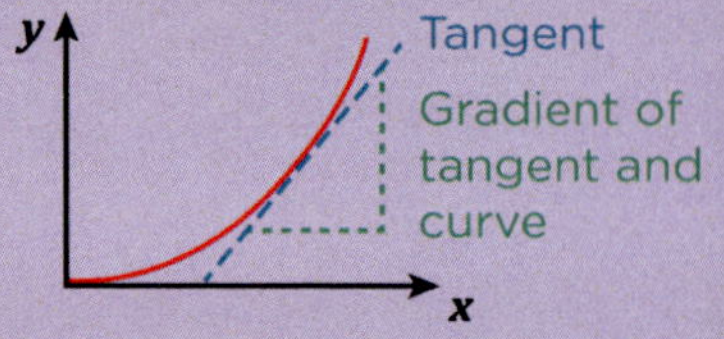

- The x or y intercept is the point where the line crosses the x or y axis.
- The **area under a line graph** is the value that corresponds to multiplying together the two variables shown in the graph as they are both changing.
  - For straight line graphs, this area can be calculated using the formula for the area of a rectangle or a triangle.
  - For curves, this area can be estimated by counting the squares beneath the graph.

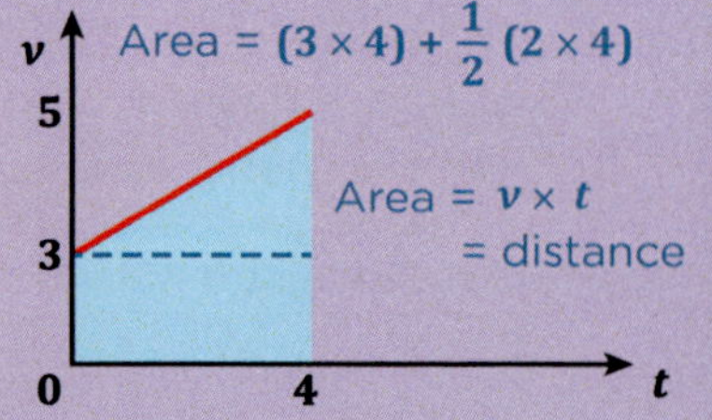

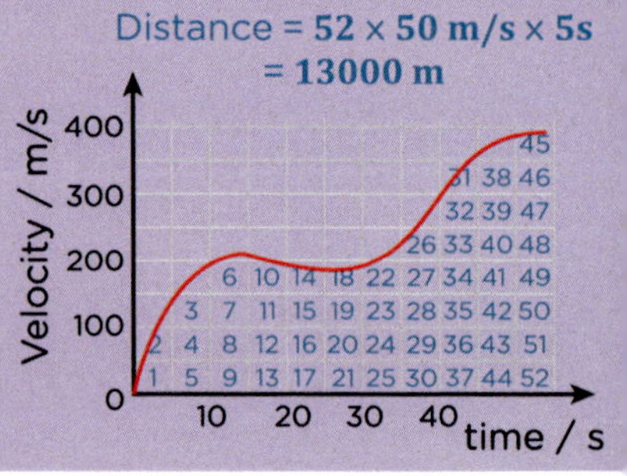